WRITING FOR BEGINNERS

VOLUME 1
NAMES FOR YOUR CHARACTERS

ANGEL BEARFIELD

NAMES FOR YOUR CHARACTERS

Just like any other author, I get stumped at times when creating names for my characters. Sometimes I will sit at my desk trying to come up with a good name for my hero/heroine and become frustrated because I couldn't come up with anything that would fit . Least of all a name that hasn't been used in several books that were recently dropped.

That's when I decided to create an extensive list of names. This will keep me from tirelessly coming up with a name only to scratch it out. Now all I do is scan through my list until I find a name that stands out to me. I highlight the name so I'm sure not to use it again in a future book. When I come across a name that I might want to add, I write it down and keep it for later.

Having a ready made list of names on hand will save you time and fill your novels with character names that stand out. Happy searching!

ANGEL

CONTENTS

WOMEN NAMES

Aaliyah
Abagail
Abbey
Abbie
Abbigail
Abby
Abigail
Abigale
Abigayle
Adaline
Addie
Addison
Adelina
Adeline
Adell
Adelle
Adena
Adina
Adria
Adrian
Adriana
Adriane
Adrianna
Adrianne
Adrien
Adriene
Adrienne
Agatha
Agnes
Agnus
Agustina
Aida
Aimee
Aisha
Aiyana
Aja
Alana
Alanna
Alayna
Alecia
Aleisha
Alesha
Aleshia
Alessandra

Alexa
Alexandra
Alexandrea
Alexandria
Alexia
Alexis
Alfreeda
Alia
Alice
Alicia
Alina
Alisa
Alise
Alisha
Alishia
Alison
Alissa
Alivia
Aliya
Aliyah
Aliza
Alleen
Allegra
Allena
Allie
Allison
Ally
Allyn
Allyson
Alona
Alondra
Althea
Alvina
Alyce
Alycia
Alysa
Alyse
Alysha
Alysia
Alyson
Alyssa
Amanda
Amani
Amara
Amari
Amaya
Amber
Amee
Amelia
Amina
Amira
Amiya
Amiyah
Ammie
Amy
Amya
Anabel
Analisa
Anamaria
Anastacia
Anastasia
Anaya

Andrea	Annemarie
Andria	Annett
Anette	Annetta
Angel	Annette
Angela	Annice
Angelena	Annie
Angelia	Annika
Angelica	Annis
Angelina	Annita
Angie	Annmarie
Anisa	Ansley
Anisha	Antionette
Anissa	Antoinette
Anita	Antonetta
Anitra	Antonette
Aniya	Anya
Aniyah	April
Anjelica	Apryl
Ann	Arabella
Anna	Aretha
Annabel	Aria
Annabell	Ariana
Annabella	Ariane
Annabelle	Arianna
Annalee	Arianne
Annalisa	Arie
Annalise	Ariel
Annamarie	Arielle
Anne	Arla
Anneliese	Arlean
Annelle	Arleen

Arlena	Bambi
Arlene	Barb
Arletta	Barbar
Arlette	Barbara
Arlinda	Barbera
Arline	Barbie
Arlyne	Barbra
Aryana	Baylee
Aryanna	Beatrice
Asha	Beatris
Ashely	Bebe
Ashlea	Becki
Ashlee	Beckie
Ashley	Becky
Ashlie	Belinda
Ashly	Bella
Ashlyn	Belle
Asia	Berenice
Audrey	Bernadette
Augustina	Bernadine
Augustine	Berneice
Autumn	Bernetta
Ava	Bernice
Avelina	Bernie
Ayana	Berniece
Ayanna	Bernita
Ayesha	Berta
Ayla	Bertha
Aylin	Bertie
Bailee	Bess
Bailey	Bessie

Beth

Bethanie

Bethany

Betsey

Betsy

Bette

Bettie

Bettina

Betty

Beula

Bev

Beverlee

Beverley

Beverly

Bianca

Billie

Blaire

Blanca

Blanch

Blanche

Bobbi

Bonnie

Brandie

Brandy

Breanne

Bree

Brenda

Brianna

Brianne

Bridget

Bridgett

Bridgette

Britany

Britney

Brittaney

Brittani

Brittanie

Brittany

Britteny

Brittney

Brook

Brooke

Bryanna

Buffy

Bunny

Cadence

Caitlin

Caitlyn

Cali

Callie

Camilla

Camille

Cammie

Cammy

Candace

Candance

Candi

Candice

Candie

Candis

Candra

Candy

Candyce
Caprice
Cara
Caren
Carey
Cari
Carie
Carin
Carina
Carisa
Carissa
Carla
Carlee
Carleen
Carlena
Carlene
Carletta
Carley
Carli
Carlie
Carline
Carlita
Carlotta
Carly
Carlyn
Carma
Carman
Carmela
Carmelia
Carmelina
Carmelita

Carmella
Carmen
Carmina
Carmon
Carol
Carolanne
Carole
Carolin
Carolina
Caroline
Caroll
Carolyn
Carolyne
Carolynn
Carri
Carrie
Carrol
Carroll
Carry
Cary
Caryl
Carylon
Caryn
Casandra
Casey
Casie
Cassandra
Cassey
Cassi
Cassie
Cassondra

Cassy
Catalina
Catarina
Caterina
Catharine
Catherin
Catherina
Catherine
Cathern
Catheryn
Cathey
Cathi
Cathie
Cathleen
Cathrine
Cathryn
Cathy
Catina
Catrice
Catrina
Cayla
Cecelia
Cecila
Cecile
Cecilia
Cecille
Cecily
Celena
Celesta
Celeste
Celestina

Celestine
Celia
Celina
Celinda
Celine
Celsa
Charleen
Charlene
Charlie
Charline
Charlotte
Charmaine
Charolette
Chelsea
Chelsey
Chelsie
Cher
Chere
Cherelle
Cheri
Cherie
Cherise
Cherish
Cherri
Cherrie
Cherry
Cherryl
Cheyanne
Cheyenne
China
Chloe

Chrissy
Christa
Christal
Christeen
Christen
Christena
Christene
Christian
Christie
Christin
Christina
Christine
Christy
Chrystal
Ciara
Ciera
Cierra
Cindie
Cindy
Cinthia
Claire
Clara
Clare
Clarice
Clarissa
Claudette
Claudia
Claudie
Claudine
Clora
Coleen

Colene
Coletta
Colette
Colleen
Collene
Collette
Connie
Constance
Contessa
Cora
Coral
Coralee
Coralie
Corazon
Cordelia
Cordia
Cordie
Coreen
Corene
Coretta
Corey
Cori
Corie
Corina
Corine
Corinna
Corinne
Corliss
Cornelia
Corrie
Corrin

Corrina
Corrine
Corrinne
Cortney
Courtney
Crissy
Cristal
Cristen
Cristie
Cristina
Cristine
Cristy
Crystal
Crystle
Cyndi
Cyndy
Cynthia
Cyrstal
Cythia
Dahlia
Daina
Daisey
Daisy
Dakota
Dalia
Dalila
Dallas
Dana
Danelle
Danette
Dani

Daniel
Daniele
Daniell
Daniella
Danielle
Danille
Danita
Dannette
Dannie
Dannielle
Danyel
Danyell
Danyelle
Daphine
Daphne
Darby
Darcey
Darci
Darcie
Darcy
Daria
Darla
Darleen
Darlena
Darlene
Darline
Dasia
Davina
Dawn
Dawna
Dawne

Dayana
Deadra
Deana
Deane
Deanna
Deanne
Deb
Debbi
Debbie
Debbra
Debby
Debera
Debi
Debora
Deborah
Debra
Debrah
Debroah
Dee
Deeanna
Deedee
Deedra
Deena
Deidra
Deidre
Deirdre
Deja
Delaine
Delana
Delcie
Delena

Delfina
Delila
Delilah
Delinda
Delisa
Della
Delma
Delois
Deloise
Delora
Deloras
Delores
Deloris
Delorse
Delphia
Delphine
Delsie
Demetra
Demetria
Demetrice
Dena
Deneen
Denese
Denice
Denise
Denisha
Denisse
Denita
Dennise
Denyse
Deonna

Desirae
Desiree
Dessie
Destinee
Destiney
Destini
Destiny
Devona
Devora
Devorah
Dia
Diana
Diane
Dianna
Dianne
Diedra
Dina
Dinorah
Dion
Dione
Dionna
Dionne
Divina
Dixie
Dollie
Dolly
Dolores
Doloris
Dominica
Dominique
Dominque

Domonique
Dona
Donella
Donetta
Donette
Donita
Donna
Donnetta
Donnette
Donya
Dora
Dorathy
Doreatha
Doreen
Dorene
Doretha
Dorethea
Dori
Dorian
Dorie
Dorinda
Dorine
Doris
Dorris
Dorthea
Dorthey
Dorthy
Dottie
Dotty
Drucilla
Drusilla

Dwana
Earlean
Earleen
Earlene
Earnestine
Eartha
Easter
Eboni
Ebonie
Ebony
Eda
Eden
Edith
Edna
Edwina
Edyth
Edythe
Effie
Eileen
Eilene
Ela
Elaina
Elaine
Elana
Elane
Elanor
Elayne
Eleanor
Eleanora
Eleanore
Elease

Elena
Elene
Elenor
Elenora
Elenore
Eleonor
Eleonora
Eleonore
Eliana
Elicia
Elina
Elinor
Elisa
Elisabeth
Elise
Elisha
Elissa
Eliza
Elizabeth
Elizbeth
Elizebeth
Ella
Ellan
Elle
Ellen
Ellena
Ellie
Ellis
Elly
Ellyn
Elma

Elmer	Erica
Elmira	Ericka
Elnora	Erika
Elois	Erin
Eloisa	Erinn
Eloise	Erlene
Elouise	Erlinda
Elsa	Erline
Elsie	Erma
Elsy	Eryn
Elvera	Esmeralda
Elvia	Essie
Elvie	Esta
Elvina	Estela
Elvira	Estell
Elwanda	Estella
Elyse	Estelle
Elyssa	Ester
Elza	Esther
Ema	Ethel
Emelia	Etta
Emelina	Ettie
Emely	Eugena
Emilee	Eugene
Emilia	Eugenia
Emilie	Eugenie
Emily	Eula
Emma	Eunice
Emmalee	Eva
Emogene	Evalyn
Enda	Evangelina

Eve
Evelin
Evelyn
Evelyne
Evelynn
Evette
Evie
Evon
Evonne
Fabiola
Fae
Faith
Fancy
Fannie
Fanny
Farah
Farrah
Fatima
Fatimah
Fay
Faye
Fe Fe
Felecia
Felica
Felice
Felicia
Felisha
Fiona
Flo
Flora
Florance

Florence
Florencia
Florene
Floretta
Fran
Francene
Frances
Francesca
Franchesca
Francie
Francine
Francis
Frederica
Fredricka
Freeda
Freida
Frieda
Gabriella
Gabrielle
Gail
Gale
Galilea
Galina
Gearldine
Gema
Gemma
Gena
Gene
Geneva
Genevieve
Genia

Genie	Giselle
Genna	Gisselle
Gennie	Gladis
Genny	Glady
Georgeann	Gladys
Georgeanna	Glenda
Georgette	Glendora
Georgia	Glinda
Georgiana	Gloria
Georgiann	Glory
Georgianna	Glynda
Georgianne	Glynis
Geraldine	Goldie
Gerda	Grace
Gerri	Gracelyn
Gerry	Gracie
Gertha	Grayce
Gertie	Greta
Gertrude	Gretchen
Gia	Gretta
Giana	Grisel
Gianna	Gwen
Gigi	Gwenda
Gillian	Gwendolyn
Gina	Gwenn
Ginette	Gwyn
Ginger	Gwyneth
Ginny	Hailey
Giovanna	Hailie
Gisela	Halie
Gisele	Halina

Halle	Holley
Halley	Hollie
Hallie	Hollis
Han	Holly
Hanna	Hope
Hannah	Hue
Harriet	Ida
Harriett	Idalia
Harriette	Iesha
Hattie	Ilana
Haydee	Ileana
Hayden	Ileen
Haylee	Ilene
Haylie	Iliana
Hazel	Ilona
Heather	Imani
Heidi	Imma
Heidy	Imogene
Helen	India
Helena	Ines
Helene	Inez
Helga	Inga
Hellen	Ingrid
Henrietta	Iola
Henriette	Iona
Hester	Ira
Hettie	Irene
Hiedi	Iris
Hilary	Irma
Hilda	Isa
Hillary	Isabel

Isabela

Isabell

Isabella

Isabelle

Isadora

Isobel

Ivana

Ivette

Ivonne

Ivory

Ivy

Iyana

Iyanna

Izabella

Jacalyn

Jacelyn

Jacinda

Jackeline

Jackelyn

Jacki

Jackie

Jacklyn

Jackqueline

Jacqualine

Jacquelin

Jacqueline

Jacquelyn

Jacquelyne

Jacquelynn

Jada

Jade

Jae

Jaelyn

Jaelynn

Jaida

Jaiden

Jaidyn

Jailyn

Jaime

Jaimee

Jaimie

Jakayla

Jaleesa

Jalisa

Jaliyah

Jalyn

Jalynn

Jamee

Jamey

Jami

Jamie

Jamika

Jamila

Jan

Jana

Janae

Janay

Jane

Janean

Janee

Janeen

Janel

Janell
Janella
Janelle
Janene
Janessa
Janet
Janeth
Janett
Janetta
Janette
Janey
Jani
Janiah
Janice
Janie
Janiece
Janina
Janine
Janis
Janise
Janita
Janiya
Janiyah
Jannet
Jannette
Janyce
Jaqueline
Jaquelyn
Jasmin
Jasmine
Jasmyn

Jaunita
Jayda
Jayla
Jaylene
Jaylin
Jaymie
Jazlyn
Jazmin
Jazmine
Jazmyn
Jeanelle
Jeanene
Jeanetta
Jeanette
Jeanice
Jeanie
Jeanmarie
Jeanna
Jeanne
Jeannetta
Jeannette
Jeannie
Jeannine
Jen
Jenee
Jenell
Jenelle
Jenette
Jenice
Jenifer
Jeniffer

Jenise
Jenna
Jennefer
Jennell
Jennette
Jenni
Jennie
Jennifer
Jenniffer
Jenny
Jeraldine
Jesica
Jessica
Jestine
Jewel
Jill
Jillian
Jin
Jina
Jinny
Jo
Joane
Joanie
Joanne
Jocelyn
Jodee
Johana
Johanna
Johanne
Joi
Jolanda

Joleen
Jolene
Jolie
Jone
Jonell
Jonelle
Joni
Jonie
Josefina
Josefine
Josephina
Josephine
Josette
Josie
Joslyn
Joy
Joyce
Juanita
Jude
Judie
Judith
Judy
Jule
Julee
Julia
Julianna
Julianne
Julie
Juliet
Julieta
Julietta

Juliette
Julissa
June
Junie
Justina
Justine
Kacey
Kacie
Kacy
Kadence
Kaelyn
Kai
Kailee
Kailey
Kailyn
Kaitlin
Kaitlyn
Kaitlynn
Kaiya
Kala
Kaley
Kali
Kaliyah
Kallie
Kalyn
Kami
Kamilah
Kandace
Kandi
Kandice
Kandis

Kandra
Kandy
Kanesha
Kanisha
Kara
Karan
Karen
Karey
Kari
Karie
Karima
Karin
Karina
Karisa
Karissa
Karla
Karlee
Karleen
Karley
Karli
Karlie
Karly
Karlyn
Karmen
Karol
Karoline
Karolyn
Karon
Karren
Karri
Karrie

Karry
Kary
Karyl
Karyn
Kasandra
Kasey
Kasi
Kasie
Kassandra
Kassidy
Kassie
Kate
Katelin
Katelyn
Katelynn
Kathaleen
Katharina
Katharine
Katharyn
Katheleen
Katherin
Katherine
Katheryn
Kathey
Kathi
Kathie
Kathleen
Kathlene
Kathlyn
Kathrin
Kathrine

Kathryn
Kathryne
Kathy
Kati
Katia
Katie
Katina
Katlyn
Katrice
Katrina
Kattie
Kay
Kayce
Kayden
Kaydence
Kaye
Kayla
Kaylah
Kaylee
Kayleen
Kayleigh
Kaylen
Kaylene
Kayley
Kayli
Kaylie
Kaylin
Kaylyn
Kaylynn
Keena
Keesha

Keira
Keisha
Kelle
Kellee
Kelley
Kelli
Kellie
Kelly
Kelsey
Kelsi
Kelsie
Kemberly
Kena
Kendal
Kendra
Kenisha
Kenna
Kennedi
Kennedy
Kenneth
Kenya
Kenyatta
Kenyetta
Kenzie
Keren
Keri
Kerri
Kerrie
Kerry
Kerstin
Kesha
Keshia
Keva
Keyla
Kia
Kiana
Kianna
Kiara
Kiera
Kierra
Kiersten
Kiesha
Kiley
Kim
Kimber
Kimberley
Kimberlie
Kimberly
Kimi
Kina
Kindra
Kinsey
Kira
Kirby
Kirsten
Kirstie
Kirstin
Kisha
Kit
Klara
Kori
Kortney

Kourtney	Laila
Krissy	Laine
Kristal	Lainey
Kristeen	Lakita
Kristen	Lala
Kristi	Lamonica
Kristie	Lana
Kristin	Lanell
Kristina	Lanelle
Kristine	Lanette
Kristy	Laney
Kristyn	Lanie
Krystal	Lanora
Krysten	Lara
Krystin	Larae
Krystina	Laraine
Kya	Laree
Kyla	Larisa
Kyle	Larissa
Kylee	Larraine
Kylie	Lashay
Kym	Lashell
Kymberly	Lashon
Kyra	Latasha
Lacey	Latashia
Lachelle	Latesha
Laci	Laticia
Lacie	Latisha
Lacresha	Latonia
Lacy	Latonya
Ladonna	Latoria

Latosha
Latoya
Latoyia
Latrice
Latricia
Latrina
Latrisha
Launa
Laura
Lauralee
Lauran
Laureen
Laurel
Lauren
Laurena
Laurene
Lauretta
Laurette
Lauri
Laurice
Laurie
Laurinda
Laurine
Lauryn
Lavelle
Lavenia
Lavera
Lavern
Laverna
Laverne
Laveta

Lavette
Lavina
Lavinia
Lavon
Lavona
Lavonda
Lavone
Lavonia
Lavonna
Lavonne
Layla
Layne
Lea
Leah
Leana
Leanna
Leanne
Leanora
Leatrice
Lecia
Leeanna
Leeanne
Leena
Leesa
Leia
Leigha
Leila
Leilani
Leisa
Leisha
Lekisha

Lela
Lelah
Lelia
Lena
Lenita
Lenna
Lenora
Lenore
Leola
Leonor
Leonora
Leonore
Lesa
Lesha
Lesia
Leslee
Lesley
Lesli
Leslie
Lesly
Leticia
Letisha
Letitia
Lettie
Letty
Lexi
Lexie
Lia
Liana
Liane
Lianne

Libbie
Libby
Lidia
Lila
Lilian
Liliana
Lillia
Lilliam
Lillian
Lilliana
Lillie
Lilly
Lily
Lin
Lina
Linda
Lindsay
Lindsey
Lindsy
Lindy
Linette
Linn
Linnea
Linsey
Lisa
Lisabeth
Lisandra
Lisbeth
Lisette
Lisha
Lissa

Lissette	Lorette
Lita	Lori
Litzy	Loria
Livia	Loriann
Liza	Lorie
Lizabeth	Lorilee
Lizbeth	Lorina
Lizette	Lorinda
Lizzette	Lorine
Lizzie	Loris
Lois	Lorita
Loise	Lorraine
Lola	Lorretta
Lolita	Lorri
Londa	Lorriane
London	Lorrie
Loni	Lorrine
Lonna	Lory
Lonnie	Lottie
Lora	Louanne
Loraine	Louella
Loralee	Louetta
Lorean	Louisa
Loree	Louise
Loreen	Loura
Loren	Lourie
Lorena	Louvenia
Lorene	Luanna
Lorenza	Luanne
Loreta	Lucia
Loretta	Luciana

Lucie
Lucila
Lucile
Lucilla
Lucille
Lucina
Lucinda
Lucrecia
Lucretia
Lucy
Luella
Luetta
Luisa
Luise
Luna
Lura
Lurlene
Lurline
Luvenia
Lydia
Lyla
Lyn
Lynda
Lyndia
Lyndsay
Lyndsey
Lynelle
Lynetta
Lynette
Lynn
Lynna

Lynne
Lynnette
Lynsey
Lyric
Mabel
Mabelle
Mable
Macey
Machelle
Maci
Macie
Macy
Madalene
Madaline
Madalyn
Madalynn
Maddie
Maddison
Madelaine
Madeleine
Madelene
Madeline
Madelyn
Madelynn
Madie
Madilyn
Madisen
Madison
Madisyn
Madlyn
Madonna

Madyson
Mae
Maegan
Magan
Magaret
Magdalen
Magdalena
Magdalene
Magen
Maggie
Mahalia
Mai
Maisha
Maisie
Majorie
Makaila
Makayla
Makeda
Makena
Makenna
Maleah
Malena
Malia
Malika
Malinda
Malisa
Malissa
Maliyah
Malka
Mallie
Mallory

Malorie
Malvina
Mammie
Manda
Mandi
Mandie
Mandy
Manie
Manuela
Maragaret
Maragret
Maranda
Marcela
Marcell
Marcella
Marcelle
Marcene
Marci
Marcia
Marcie
Marcy
Margaret
Margareta
Margarete
Margarett
Margaretta
Margarette
Margarita
Margarite
Marge
Margeret

Margie	Marina
Margo	Marinda
Margorie	Marisa
Margot	Marisha
Margret	Marisol
Margrett	Marissa
Marguerite	Marjorie
Margurite	Marjory
Margy	Marketta
Marhta	Markita
Maria	Marla
Mariah	Marlana
Mariam	Marleen
Marian	Marlena
Mariana	Marlene
Marianna	Marquetta
Marianne	Marquita
Maribel	Marquitta
Maribeth	Marry
Maricela	Marsha
Marie	Marta
Mariel	Martha
Mariela	Martina
Mariella	Mary
Marielle	Maryam
Marietta	Maryann
Mariette	Maryanna
Marilee	Maryanne
Marilou	Marybelle
Marilyn	Marybeth
Marilynn	Maryellen

Maryetta	Melba
Maryjane	Melia
Marylee	Melina
Marylin	Melinda
Maryln	Melisa
Marylou	Melissa
Marylyn	Melissia
Marylynn	Mellie
Matilda	Mellisa
Mattie	Mellissa
Maud	Melodee
Maude	Melodi
Maureen	Melodie
Maurine	Melody
Maurita	Melonie
Maxie	Melony
Maxine	Melynda
May	Mendy
Maybelle	Meredith
Maye	Merideth
Mckayla	Meridith
Mckenna	Merilyn
Meagan	Merissa
Meaghan	Merlene
Mechelle	Merlyn
Megan	Merri
Meggan	Merrie
Meghan	Merrilee
Melani	Merry
Melanie	Mertie
Melany	Meryl

Mia
Miah
Micaela
Michele
Michelina
Michell
Michelle
Mikaela
Mikayla
Mildred
Miley
Milissa
Millicent
Millie
Milly
Mimi
Mina
Mindi
Mindy
Minnie
Mira
Miracle
Miranda
Miriam
Mirian
Misha
Miya
Mollie
Molly
Mona
Monet

Monica
Monika
Monique
Monnie
Moriah
Muriel
Mya
Myah
Myesha
Myra
Myriam
Myrtle
Nadene
Nadia
Nadine
Nakesha
Nakia
Nakisha
Nakita
Nan
Nancee
Nancey
Nanci
Nancie
Nancy
Nanette
Nannette
Naoma
Naomi
Natacha
Natalee

Natalia
Natalie
Nataly
Natalya
Natasha
Natashia
Natisha
Natosha
Necole
Nedra
Neely
Neida
Nelda
Nelia
Nell
Nelle
Nellie
Nelly
Nena
Neomi
Nerissa
Netta
Nettie
Neva
Nevada
Nevaeh
Nevaeh (heaven spelled backwards)
Nia
Nichelle
Nichole
Nicholle
Nicki
Nickie
Nickole
Nicky
Nicol
Nicola
Nicole
Nicolette
Nicolle
Nida
Nidia
Niesha
Niki
Nikia
Nikita
Nikki
Nikole
Nila
Nilsa
Nina
Nisha
Nita
Noel
Noella
Noelle
Nola
Nora
Norah
Noreen
Norene

Norine
Norma
Nya
Nyah
Nyasia
Nydia
Nyla
Octavia
Odessa
Odilia
Ofelia
Olga
Olinda
Olivia
Ollie
Opal
Ophelia
Oretha
Paige
Pam
Pamala
Pamela
Pamelia
Pamella
Pamila
Pamula
Paris
Particia
Pat
Patience
Patrice

Patricia
Patrina
Patsy
Patti
Pattie
Patty
Paula
Paulene
Pauletta
Paulette
Paulina
Pauline
Pearl
Pearle
Pearlene
Pearline
Peg
Peggie
Peggy
Penelope
Penni
Pennie
Penny
Perry
Petrina
Phebe
Phillis
Philomena
Phoebe
Phoenix
Phylicia

Phylis
Phyliss
Phyllis
Piper
Polly
Presley
Pricilla
Priscila
Priscilla
Prudence
Qiana
Quinn
Rachael
Rachal
Racheal
Rachel
Rachele
Rachell
Rachelle
Racquel
Raeann
Raina
Ramona
Ranae
Randee
Randi
Randy
Ranee
Raquel
Raven
Raye

Raylene
Rayna
Reanna
Reatha
Reba
Rebbeca
Rebbecca
Rebeca
Rebecca
Rebecka
Rebekah
Reena
Regena
Regenia
Regina
Regine
Reginia
Reina
Remona
Rena
Renae
Renay
Renda
Rene
Renee
Renetta
Renita
Retta
Reva
Reyna
Rhea

Rheba
Rhianna
Rhoda
Rhonda
Ria
Richelle
Rihanna
Rima
Rina
Risa
Rita
Robbin
Robbyn
Robin
Robyn
Rochel
Rochell
Rochelle
Rolanda
Romona
Ronda
Ronnie
Rory
Rosa
Rosalee
Rosalia
Rosalie
Rosalina
Rosalind
Rosalinda
Rosaline

Rosalyn
Rosamaria
Rosana
Rosanna
Rosanne
Rose
Roseanna
Roseanne
Roselee
Roselia
Rosella
Roselyn
Rosemarie
Rosemary
Rosena
Rosenda
Rosetta
Rosette
Rosia
Rosie
Rosina
Roslyn
Rossie
Rosy
Roxana
Roxane
Roxann
Roxanna
Roxanne
Roxie
Roxy

Rozanne	Sandie
Rozella	Sandra
Rubi	Sandy
Rubie	Saniya
Ruby	Saniyah
Ruth	Sanora
Ruthe	Sara
Ruthie	Sarah
Rylee	Sarai
Rylie	Sari
Sabrina	Sariah
Sacha	Sarina
Sade	Sarita
Sadie	Sasha
Sadye	Saundra
Saige	Savana
Salena	Savanah
Salina	Savanna
Salley	Savannah
Sallie	Scarlet
Sally	Scarlett
Sam	Sebrina
Samantha	Selena
Samara	Selene
Samatha	Selina
Samella	Selma
Samira	Serena
Sammie	Serenity
Sammy	Serina
Sandee	Serita
Sandi	Shala

Shalonda
Shameka
Shamika
Shan
Shana
Shanae
Shanda
Shandra
Shanel
Shanell
Shanelle
Shani
Shania
Shanice
Shanika
Shanita
Shaniya
Shanna
Shannan
Shannon
Shanon
Shanta
Shantae
Shantay
Shante
Shantel
Shantell
Shantelle
Shanti
Shara
Sharan

Sharee
Sharell
Sharen
Shari
Sharice
Sharie
Sharika
Sharilyn
Sharita
Sharla
Sharleen
Sharlene
Sharmaine
Sharon
Sharonda
Sharri
Sharron
Sharyl
Sharyn
Shauna
Shaunda
Shaunna
Shaunte
Shavon
Shavonda
Shavonne
Shawanda
Shawna
Shawnna
Shay
Shayla

Shaylee
Shayna
Shayne
Shea
Sheba
Sheena
Sheila
Sheilah
Shela
Shelba
Shelby
Shelia
Shella
Shelley
Shelli
Shellie
Shelly
Shemeka
Shemika
Shena
Shenika
Shenita
Shenna
Shera
Sheree
Sherell
Sheri
Sherice
Sherie
Sherika
Sherill
Sherilyn
Sherise
Sherita
Sherlene
Sherley
Sherly
Sherlyn
Sheron
Sherrell
Sherri
Sherrie
Sherril
Sherrill
Sherron
Sherry
Sherryl
Shery
Sheryl
Sheryll
Shiela
Shira
Shirely
Shirl
Shirlee
Shirleen
Shirlene
Shirley
Shirly
Shona
Shonda
Shondra

Shyann	Stacey
Shyanne	Staci
Shyla	Stacie
Sibyl	Stacy
Siena	Stasia
Sienna	Stefani
Sierra	Stefanie
Silva	Stefany
Silvana	Steffanie
Silvia	Stella
Simona	Stephaine
Simone	Stephani
Simonne	Stephania
Sindy	Stephanie
Sirena	Stephany
Sky	Stephenie
Skye	Stephnie
Skyla	Suanne
Skylar	Sue
Skyler	Sue-Ellen
Slyvia	Summer
Sofia	Sunny
Sommer	Susan
Sondra	Susana
Sonia	Susann
Sonja	Susanna
Sonya	Susannah
Sophia	Susanne
Sophie	Susie
Soraya	Susy
Stacee	Suzan

Suzann	Tami
Suzanna	Tamia
Suzanne	Tamica
Suzette	Tamie
Suzie	Tamika
Sybil	Tamisha
Syble	Tammara
Sydni	Tammera
Sydnie	Tammi
Sylvia	Tammie
Sylvie	Tammy
Synthia	Tandra
Tabatha	Tandy
Tabetha	Taneka
Tabitha	Tanesha
Tai	Tangela
Taisha	Tania
Takisha	Tanika
Talia	Tanisha
Talisha	Taniya
Talitha	Taniyah
Taliyah	Tanja
Tamala	Tanna
Tamar	Tanya
Tamara	Tara
Tamatha	Tarah
Tameika	Taren
Tameka	Tari
Tamekia	Taryn
Tamera	Tasha
Tamesha	Tashia

Tashina
Tasia
Tatiana
Tatyana
Tawana
Tawanda
Tawanna
Tawnya
Tayler
Taylor
Tayna
Teena
Teisha
Temeka
Temika
Tena
Tenesha
Tenisha
Tera
Tereasa
Teresa
Terese
Teresia
Teresita
Teressa
Teri
Terina
Terisa
Terra
Terresa
Terri

Terrie
Terry
Tesha
Tess
Tessa
Tessie
Thalia
Thea
Thelma
Theodora
Theola
Theresa
Therese
Theresia
Theressa
Thomasena
Thomasina
Thomasine
Thora
Tia
Tiana
Tianna
Tiara
Tiera
Tierra
Tiesha
Tifany
Tiffaney
Tiffani
Tiffanie
Tiffany

Tiffiny
Tillie
Tilly
Timika
Tina
Tinisha
Tisa
Tish
Tisha
Tomeka
Tomika
Tonda
Tonette
Toni
Tonia
Tonie
Tonisha
Tonita
Tonja
Tonya
Tora
Tori
Torie
Torri
Torrie
Tory
Tosha
Toshia
Towanda
Toya
Tracee

Tracey
Traci
Tracie
Tracy
Treasa
Treena
Tressa
Tressie
Tricia
Trina
Trinity
Trish
Trisha
Trista
Trudy
Twana
Twanda
Twanna
Tyesha
Tyisha
Tynisha
Tyra
Ula
Ursula
Val
Valarie
Valencia
Valeri
Valerie
Valery
Valorie

Vanesa
Vanessa
Vanetta
Vanita
Vanna
Vannesa
Vannessa
Veda
Velda
Vella
Velma
Vena
Venessa
Venetta
Venice
Venita
Venus
Veola
Vera
Verda
Verdie
Verla
Verlene
Verline
Vernice
Vernita
Veronica
Veronika
Vesta
Veta
Vickey

Vicki
Vickie
Vicky
Victoria
Vida
Viki
Vikki
Vinita
Viola
Violet
Violette
Virginia
Vita
Vivian
Viviana
Vivien
Vivienne
Vonda
Vonnie
Wanda
Waneta
Wanetta
Wanita
Wendi
Wendie
Wendolyn
Wendy
Wenona
Whitley
Whitney
Wilhelmina

Wilhemina
Willetta
Willette
Willow
Wilma
Windy
Winifred
Winnie
Winnifred
Winona
Winter
Wonda
Wynona
Xenia
Yadira
Yahaira
Yanira
Yasmin
Yasmine
Yazmin
Yelena
Yevette
Yolanda
Yolonda
Yulanda
Yuri
Yvette
Yvonne
Zada
Zandra
Zara

Zaria
Zariah
Zelda
Zella
Zelma
Zena
Zetta
Zina
Zoe
Zoey
Zofia
Zola
Zonia
Zora
Zulema

MEN NAMES

Aaren
Aaron
Abbott
Abdul
Abdullah
Abe
Abel
Abraham
Abram
Adair
Adam
Addison
Aden
Adreian
Adrian
Adrien
Adrion
Agustin

Ahmad
Ahmed
Aidan
Aiden
Aiken
Aikin
Ajay
Al
Alan
Alastair
Albert
Alberto
Alburt
Alec
Alejandro
Alen
Alex
Alexander

Alexandro
Alexzander
Alfonse
Alfonso
Alfonzo
Alford
Alfred
Ali
Alijah
Alistair
Allan
Allen
Allin
Allon
Alonso
Alonzo
Alphonse
Alphonso
Alphonzo
Alton
Alvin
Amari
Amir
Amos
Anderson
Andre
Andrew
Andy
Angel
Angelo
Anthony

Antione
Antoine
Anton
Antonio
Antony
Antwan
Archibald
Archie
Arlen
Arlie
Arnold
Arthur
Arwin
Ashton
Aston
Augustine
Augustus
Austen
Austin
Aven
Avery
Axel
Aydan
Ayden
Aydin
Bain
Baine
Bane
Barney
Barnie
Barny

Barry
Bart
Bartholemew
Bartholomew
Baylin
Bayne
Beck
Ben
Benedict
Benet
Benjamin
Benny
Benson
Bernard
Bernie
Berry
Bert
Bill
Billie
Billy
Blake
Bo
Bob
Bobbie
Bobby
Boris
Brad
Branden
Brandon
Braxton
Brenden

Brendon
Brendt
Brian
Briant
Brice
Broddy
Broderic
Broderick
Bruce
Bryan
Bryant
Bryce
Bryceton
Bryson
Bryston
Buford
Burt
Byran
Byron
Cace
Cacey
Cade
Caden
Caelan
Caesar
Caeser
Cahil
Cahir
Caiden
Caidin
Caidon

Cailin
Cain
Caine
Cal
Calan
Calbert
Caldwell
Cale
Caleb
Calen
Calhaun
Calhoun
Calin
Calix
Callhoun
Callum
Calum
Calvin
Calvyn
Camaron
Cameron
Camillo
Camillus
Camilo
Camilus
Camren
Camron
Cannon
Carl
Carlos
Carlton

Carlyle
Carmelo
Carmen
Carmine
Carsen
Carson
Carter
Cason
Cassius
Castor
Cayden
Cecil
Cedric
Cedrick
Cesar
Chad
Chadwick
Chance
Chandler
Channing
Charles
Charley
Charlie
Chase
Chauncey
Chaz
Chester
Chet
Chip
Chris
Christian

Christoper
Christopher
Chuck
Clarence
Clark
Clarke
Claud
Claude
Clay
Clayton
Clement
Clemente
Cleo
Cletus
Cliff
Clifford
Clifton
Clint
Clinton
Clive
Clyde
Coby
Cohen
Colby
Cole
Coleman
Colin
Collin
Columbus
Conner
Connor

Conor
Conrad
Constantine
Corbin
Cordell
Corey
Cornelius
Cornell
Cory
Courtney
Craig
Cristian
Cristofer
Cristopher
Cullen
Curt
Curtis
Cyrus
D'Shawn
Daimen
Daine
Dainel
Daire
Daiton
Daivid
Dakairi
Dakari
Dakarri
Dalbert
Dalburt
Dale

Daley	Darrell
Dallen	Darren
Dallin	Darrick
Dallon	Darrin
Dalton	Darrius
Damarion	Darron
Damian	Darryl
Damien	Darryn
Damion	Darwin
Damon	Daryl
Dan	Dashawn
Dandre	Dave
Dane	Davian
Danial	David
Daniel	Davin
Dannie	Davion
Danny	Davis
Dante	Davon
Daquan	Dawson
Darell	Dayton
Daren	Deacon
Darian	Dean
Darien	Deandre
Darin	Deangelo
Dario	Del
Darion	Delbert
Darius	Delmar
Darnell	Delmer
Daron	Delvin
Darran	Demarcus
Darrel	Demarion

Demetrius
Den
Denis
Dennis
Denny
Denver
Denzel
Deon
Deonte
Derek
Derick
Derik
Deron
Derrick
Deshaun
Deshawn
Desmond
Destin
Devan
Deven
Devin
Devlin
Devon
Devonte
Devyn
Dewayne
Dewey
Dex
Dexter
Dick
Diego

Dilan
Dillan
Dillon
Dimitri
Dion
Dirk
Dmitri
Domenic
Domenico
Domingo
Dominic
Dominick
Dominik
Dominique
Domonic
Don
Donald
Donavan
Donn
Donnell
Donnie
Donny
Donovan
Donte
Dorian
Dorien
Dorsey
Doug
Douglas
Douglass
Doyle

Drake
Drew
Drummond
Drummund
Drumond
Drumund
Duane
Dudlee
Dudley
Dudly
Dugan
Duglass
Duke
Duncan
Dunstan
Dunsten
Dunstin
Dunston
Dunstyn
Duran
Durand
Durandt
Durant
Durwin
Dushawn
Dustain
Dustan
Dustin
Duwayne
Dwain
Dwaine

Dwalin
Dwane
Dwayne
Dwhite
Dwight
Dwite
Dwyte
Dylan
Dyllan
Dyllon
Dylon
Earl
Earnest
Ebenezer
Ed
Eddie
Eddison
Eddy
Eden
Edgar
Edgard
Edger
Edisen
Edison
Edmon
Edmond
Edmun
Edmund
Edric
Eduard
Eduardo

Edward
Edwen
Edwin
Edwon
Edwyn
Edyson
Egan
Elden
Eldon
Eldridge
Eli
Elijah
Eliot
Elliot
Elliott
Ellis
Ellsworth
Elmer
Elroy
Elton
Elvin
Elvis
Elwood
Emanuel
Emerson
Emet
Emil
Emile
Emmanuel
Emmerson
Emmet

Emmett
Emmitt
Enrique
Eric
Erick
Erik
Ernest
Ernie
Ervin
Erwin
Esteban
Estevan
Ethan
Ethen
Eugene
Eustace
Evan
Everett
Fabain
Fabian
Farel
Farlay
Farley
Farlie
Farly
Federico
Felipe
Felix
Ferguson
Fernando
Finley

Fletcher	Gavyn
Floyd	Gene
Forrest	Geoffrey
Frances	George
Frank	Gerald
Frankie	Germain
Franklin	Gerry
Franklyn	Gideon
Fraser	Gilbert
Fred	Gino
Freddie	Giorgio
Freddy	Glen
Frederic	Glenn
Frederick	Glynn
Frederico	Gordie
Fredric	Gordon
Fredrick	Gordy
Gabe	Graham
Gabriel	Graig
Garett	Grant
Garette	Greg
Garfield	Gregg
Garret	Gregor
Garrett	Gregory
Garrison	Griffin
Garry	Gus
Garth	Hal
Gary	Halbert
Gaston	Halburt
Gaven	Hank
Gavin	Harley

Harold	Idriece
Harrison	Idris
Harry	Igor
Harvey	Ike
Hayden	Imanual
Heath	Imanuel
Hector	Immanual
Hendrick	Immanuel
Hendrik	Irvin
Henri	Irving
Henry	Irwin
Herb	Isaac
Herbert	Isaak
Herbie	Isai
Herman	Isaiah
Hollis	Isiah
Homer	Issac
Horace	Ivan
Howard	Izaiah
Howie	Jabari
Hoyt	Jabarie
Hubert	Jabarri
Hue	Jabarrie
Huey	Jabe
Hugh	Jabien
Hugo	Jabir
Humphrey	Jaccob
Humphry	Jace
Ian	Jack
Idrease	Jackques
Idrees	Jacksen

Jackson	Javier
Jacob	Javion
Jacobb	Javon
Jadan	Jayce
Jaden	Jayden
Jadin	Jaydin
Jadon	Jaydon
Jadyn	Jaylan
Jaiden	Jaylen
Jaime	Jaylin
Jake	Jaylon
Jalen	Jayson
Jamal	Jean
Jamar	Jed
Jamari	Jedidiah
Jamel	Jeff
James	Jefferey
Jameson	Jeffery
Jamir	Jeffrey
Jamison	Jeffry
Jared	Jem
Jarod	Jemir
Jarred	Jeramy
Jarrett	Jeremiah
Jarrod	Jeremy
Jarvis	Jermaine
Jase	Jerome
Jason	Jeromy
Jasper	Jerrell
Javan	Jerrod
Javen	Jerrold

Jerry	Josh
Jesse	Joshua
Jessie	Josiah
Jim	Jospeh
Jimmy	Jovan
Jodie	Juan
Jody	Julian
Joe	Julien
Joedee	Julious
Joel	Julius
Joelle	Justin
Joesph	Kade
Joey	Kaid
John	Kale
Johnathan	Kaleb
Johnathon	Kamari
Johnnie	Kamden
Johnny	Kameron
Jon	Kaone
Jonah	Karl
Jonas	Karson
Jonathan	Kasey
Jonathon	Keagan
Jordan	Kean
Jorden	Keanu
Jordon	Keaton
Jordyn	Keegan
Jorge	Keenan
Jose	Keith
Josef	Kelley
Joseph	Kelly

Kelton
Kelvin
Ken
Kendall
Kendrick
Keneth
Kenn
Kennedy
Kenneth
Kennith
Kenny
Kent
Kenton
Kenyon
Keon
Keshawn
Kev
Keven
Kevin
Kevon
Keyon
Keyshawn
Khalid
Khalil
Kieth
Kip
Kirby
Kirk
Kobe
Koby
Kody

Kolby
Kole
Konner
Konnor
Korbin
Korey
Kory
Kraig
Kris
Kristian
Kristofer
Kristopher
Kurt
Kurtis
Kylar
Kyle
Kyler
Lamar
Lambert
Lamont
Lance
Lander
Landon
Langdon
Langford
Langley
Langstan
Langsten
Langston
Lanny
Larry

Latrell
Laurence
Lawerence
Lawrence
Lawson
Lazaro
Leandro
Lee
Leland
Len
Lenard
Lennie
Lennox
Lenny
Leo
Leon
Leonard
Leonardo
Leroy
Les
Lester
Levi
Lewis
Lex
Liam
Lincoln
Lindon
Linus
Lionel
Lloyd
Logan

Lonnie
Lonny
Lorence
Lorenzo
Lou
Louie
Louis
Loyd
Lucas
Lucian
Luciano
Luis
Lukas
Luke
Luther
Lyle
Mac Kinley
Macauley
Mack
Mackenzie
Mackey
Malachi
Malaki
Malcolm
Malcom
Malik
Manual
Manuel
Marc
Marcel
Marcelino

Marcellus
Marcelo
Marco
Marcos
Marcus
Mariano
Mario
Marion
Mark
Markus
Marley
Marlin
Marlon
Marques
Marquez
Marquis
Marquise
Marshal
Marshall
Martin
Marty
Martyn
Marvin
Mat
Mateo
Mathew
Matt
Matteo
Matthew
Matty
Maurice

Maury
Max
Maximilian
Maximillian
Maximus
Maxwell
Mekhi
Mel
Melvin
Merlin
Merril
Merrill
Mervin
Mica
Micah
Michael
Michal
Micheal
Mick
Miguel
Mike
Mikel
Mikey
Miles
Milton
Miquel
Mitch
Mitchel
Mitchell
Mitt
Moe

Monroe
Monte
Monty
Morey
Morgan
Morris
Morton
Moses
Munroe
Murphy
Murray
Murry
Myles
Mylo
Myron
Nash
Nasir
Nate
Nathan
Nathanael
Nathanial
Nathaniel
Nathen
Neal
Ned
Neil
Nelson
Neville
Newton
Nicholas
Nick

Nickolas
Nicky
Nico
Nicolas
Nigel
Nik
Niko
Nikolas
Nile
Noah
Nolan
Norbert
Norbet
Norman
Norris
Ocatavious
Odell
Oliver
Ollie
Omar
Omari
Omarion
Oren
Orlando
Orville
Oscar
Oswald
Otis
Owen
Owin
Ozzie

<table>
<tr><td>Ozzy</td><td>Quentin</td></tr>
<tr><td>Pablo</td><td>Quenton</td></tr>
<tr><td>Pacey</td><td>Quill</td></tr>
<tr><td>Palmer</td><td>Quince</td></tr>
<tr><td>Patrick</td><td>Quincey</td></tr>
<tr><td>Paul</td><td>Quincy</td></tr>
<tr><td>Pauley</td><td>Quinn</td></tr>
<tr><td>Paxton</td><td>Quinten</td></tr>
<tr><td>Payce</td><td>Quintin</td></tr>
<tr><td>Payton</td><td>Quinton</td></tr>
<tr><td>Pearce</td><td>Rafe</td></tr>
<tr><td>Pedro</td><td>Ralph</td></tr>
<tr><td>Percival</td><td>Ramiro</td></tr>
<tr><td>Percy</td><td>Ramon</td></tr>
<tr><td>Perry</td><td>Ramsey</td></tr>
<tr><td>Petar</td><td>Randal</td></tr>
<tr><td>Pete</td><td>Randall</td></tr>
<tr><td>Peter</td><td>Randell</td></tr>
<tr><td>Peyton</td><td>Randolph</td></tr>
<tr><td>Phil</td><td>Randy</td></tr>
<tr><td>Philip</td><td>Raphael</td></tr>
<tr><td>Philippe</td><td>Raul</td></tr>
<tr><td>Phillip</td><td>Ray</td></tr>
<tr><td>Pierce</td><td>Raymon</td></tr>
<tr><td>Pierre</td><td>Raymond</td></tr>
<tr><td>Preston</td><td>Raymundo</td></tr>
<tr><td>Quade</td><td>Reece</td></tr>
<tr><td>Quaid</td><td>Reed</td></tr>
<tr><td>Quaide</td><td>Reese</td></tr>
<tr><td>Quent</td><td>Reggie</td></tr>
<tr><td>Quenten</td><td>Reginald</td></tr>
</table>

Reid
Remington
Renaldo
Reuben
Rey
Reynaldo
Rhett
Ricardo
Richard
Richie
Rick
Rickey
Rickie
Ricky
Rico
Riley
Rio
Rob
Robbie
Robby
Robert
Roberto
Robin
Rod
Roderic
Roderick
Rodger
Rodney
Rodrick
Roger
Roland

Rolland
Roman
Ron
Ronald
Ronaldo
Ronnie
Ronny
Roscoe
Ross
Rowan
Roy
Royce
Ruben
Rubin
Rudy
Rueben
Rupert
Russel
Russell
Ryan
Rylan
Ryland
Salvador
Salvadore
Sam
Samir
Sammie
Sammy
Sampson
Samson
Samual

Samuel
Sanford
Santiago
Santino
Santos
Saul
Savion
Sawyer
Sayvion
Scott
Scottie
Scotty
Sean
Sebastian
Sebastien
Sergio
Seth
Seymour
Shaun
Shaw
Shawn
Shayne
Sheldon
Shelton
Sherman
Sherwin
Shiloh
Sidney
Silas
Simeon
Simon

Slade
Sol
Solomon
Stacey
Stacy
Stan
Stanley
Stefan
Steffan
Stephan
Stephen
Stephon
Steve
Steven
Stevie
Stew
Stewart
Stuart
Sy
Sydney
Sylvester
T'Marius
Tad
Talan
Talon
Tanner
Tariq
Tate
Taylor
Ted
Teddy

Terence	Torry
Terrance	Tory
Terrell	Tracey
Terrence	Tracy
Terry	Tramaine
Tevin	Travis
Thaddeus	Travon
Theo	Travus
Theodore	Tremaine
Thomas	Tremane
Thurman	Tremayne
Tiberius	Trent
Tim	Trenton
Timmy	Trever
Timothy	Trevion
Tito	Trevon
Tivan	Trevor
Tivon	Trey
Tobias	Treyden
Tod	Tristan
Todd	Tristen
Tom	Tristian
Tomas	Tristin
Tommie	Triston
Tommy	Troy
Tony	Truman
Torey	Trystan
Tori	Tucker
Torin	Turner
Torrance	Ty
Torrey	Tylan

Tyler
Tylor
Tyree
Tyrell
Tyrese
Tyron
Tyrone
Tyshawn
Tyson
Uriah
Vance
Vaughn
Vence
Vergil
Vernon
Vic
Vick
Victor
Vince
Vincent
Vinnie
Vinny
Virgil
Vito
Vladimir
Von
Wade
Waldo
Wallace
Wallie
Wally

Walt
Walter
Walton
Warren
Wayne
Weldon
Wendell
Wes
Wesley
West
Westin
Weston
Wilber
Wilbert
Wilbur
Wiley
Wilford
Wilfred
Will
Willard
William
Willie
Willis
Wilson
Wilt
Wilton
Winford
Winston
Wolfe
Worrin
Wyatt

Wynston
Wynton
Xander
Xavier
Xavion
Yasir
Yorick
York
Zac
Zach
Zachariah
Zachary
Zachery
Zack
Zackary
Zackery
Zander
Zavier
Zayden
Zeke
Zontae
Zontay

LAST NAMES

Acker	Albrecht
Ackerman	Albright
Ackley	Alden
Acosta	Alderman
Acton	Alderson
Adair	Aldrich
Adams	Aldridge
Adamson	Alexander
Adcock	Alfaro
Addington	Alford
Addison	Alger
Adkins	Ali
Agee	Allard
Agnew	Allerton
Aguilar	Alley
Aguilera	Allis
Aguirre	Allred
Aiken	Alston
Ainsworth	Altizer
Aken	Altman
Akers	Alvarado
Akin	Alvarez
Akins	Alvord
Albertson	Ambrose
Albin	Ames

Amica	Ash
Amons	Ashbaugh
Amos	Ashby
Anders	Ashcraft
Andersen	Asher
Anderson	Ashworth
Andrade	Aston
Andrews	Atherton
Andrus	Atkins
Angleterre	Atkinson
Angus	Atwater
Annis	Atwood
Anthony	Aubigny
Applegate	Audley
Appling	Ault
Aquino	Austin
Aragon	Autry
Archer	Avalos
Archibald	Avery
Arellano	Avila
Arias	Aviles
Arledge	Ayer
Armstrong	Ayers
Arnett	Ayres
Arnold	Babb
Arredondo	Babcock
Arrington	Babin
Arroyo	Baca
Arthur	Bachman
Arundel	Back
Asbury	Backus

Bacon	Barling
Badger	Barlow
Badlesmere	Barmore
Baer	Barnard
Baez	Barner
Bagley	Barnes
Bailey	Barnett
Baily	Barnhart
Bain	Barnhill
Baird	Barns
Baker	Barnum
Balch	Baron
Baldwin	Barr
Bales	Barrera
Balfour	Barrett
Ballard	Barrino
Ballinger	Barrios
Ballou	Barron
Bancroft	Barrow
Bandy	Barrows
Bangs	Barry
Banks	Barstow
Banner	Bartlett
Banta	Bartley
Barajas	Barton
Barber	Barwick
Barbour	Bass
Barger	Basset
Baril	Bassett
Barker	Bastos
Barkley	Batchelor

Bate
Bateman
Bates
Battle
Bauer
Baugh
Baughman
Baum
Bauman
Bautista
Baxter
Bayley
Beach
Beal
Beale
Beam
Beaman
Bean
Bear
Beard
Beardsley
Beasley
Beattie
Beatty
Beaty
Beauchamp
Beaufort
Beaumont
Beaver
Beavers
Becerra

Beck
Becker
Beckett
Beckwith
Bedford
Bee
Beebe
Beecher
Beekman
Beers
Beery
Belanger
Belcher
Belden
Belding
Belk
Belknap
Bell
Bellamy
Belle
Bellinger
Bellingham
Bellows
Beltran
Bemis
Benavides
Bender
Benedict
Benham
Benitez
Benjamin

Benner
Bennet
Bennett
Benoit
Benson
Bent
Bentley
Benton
Berg
Bergen
Berger
Bergeron
Bergman
Berkeley
Berman
Bermudez
Bernal
Bernard
Bernier
Bernstein
Berry
Bertram
Bertrand
Best
Betts
Bevier
Beyer
Bible
Bickford
Bicknell
Biddle

Bidwell
Bigelow
Biggs
Bill
Billings
Billingsley
Bills
Bingham
Binkley
Birch
Bird
Birdwell
Bishop
Bissell
Bisson
Bivens
Bixby
Black
Blackburn
Blackman
Blackmon
Blackwell
Blackwood
Blair
Blaisdell
Blake
Blakney
Blalock
Blanchard
Blanchfield
Blanco

<table>
<tr><td>Bland</td><td>Bonner</td></tr>
<tr><td>Blankenship</td><td>Bonney</td></tr>
<tr><td>Blanton</td><td>Booker</td></tr>
<tr><td>Blaylock</td><td>Bookout</td></tr>
<tr><td>Bledsoe</td><td>Boon</td></tr>
<tr><td>Blevins</td><td>Boone</td></tr>
<tr><td>Bliss</td><td>Booth</td></tr>
<tr><td>Block</td><td>Boozer</td></tr>
<tr><td>Bloom</td><td>Borden</td></tr>
<tr><td>Blosser</td><td>Boring</td></tr>
<tr><td>Blount</td><td>Born</td></tr>
<tr><td>Blue</td><td>Borton</td></tr>
<tr><td>Blum</td><td>Boss</td></tr>
<tr><td>Blunt</td><td>Boston</td></tr>
<tr><td>Boardman</td><td>Bostwick</td></tr>
<tr><td>Bobbitt</td><td>Boswell</td></tr>
<tr><td>Bobo</td><td>Bosworth</td></tr>
<tr><td>Bogart</td><td>Boteler</td></tr>
<tr><td>Boggs</td><td>Botting</td></tr>
<tr><td>Bohun</td><td>Bouchard</td></tr>
<tr><td>Bois</td><td>Boucher</td></tr>
<tr><td>Bolden</td><td>Boudreaux</td></tr>
<tr><td>Boles</td><td>Bourchier</td></tr>
<tr><td>Bolin</td><td>Bourgeois</td></tr>
<tr><td>Bollinger</td><td>Bourne</td></tr>
<tr><td>Bolton</td><td>Bouton</td></tr>
<tr><td>Bomar</td><td>Bowden</td></tr>
<tr><td>Bond</td><td>Bowen</td></tr>
<tr><td>Bone</td><td>Bower</td></tr>
<tr><td>Bonham</td><td>Bowerman</td></tr>
<tr><td>Bonilla</td><td>Bowers</td></tr>
</table>

Bowes
Bowie
Bowker
Bowles
Bowling
Bowman
Bowne
Bowser
Box
Boyce
Boyd
Boyden
Boyer
Boykin
Boyle
Boyles
Boynton
Brace
Bradbury
Braden
Bradford
Bradley
Bradshaw
Bradstreet
Brady
Bragg
Brainard
Brainerd
Braley
Brame
Branch

Brand
Brandenburg
Brandon
Brandt
Branham
Brannon
Branson
Brantley
Braose
Brashears
Braswell
Bratton
Braun
Bravo
Bray
Breed
Breeden
Brennan
Brenneman
Brent
Brereton
Brett
Brewer
Brewster
Bridge
Bridges
Brien
Briggs
Brigham
Bright
Brink

Brinkley
Brinson
Briscoe
Bristol
Britt
Brittain
Britton
Brock
Brockman
Brockway
Bromley
Bronson
Brooke
Brooks
Brothers
Broughton
Broussard
Brower
Brown
Browne
Browning
Brubaker
Bruce
Brumfield
Bruner
Brunner
Bruno
Brunson
Brus
Brush
Bryan

Bryant
Bryson
Buchanan
Bucher
Buck
Buckingham
Buckley
Buckman
Buckner
Budd
Buell
Buffington
Buford
Bui
Bulkeley
Bull
Bullard
Bullock
Bunch
Bundy
Bunker
Bunn
Bunnell
Bunton
Burbank
Burch
Burchett
Burchfield
Burden
Burdett
Burdick

<table>
<tr><td>

Buren
Burge
Burger
Burgess
Burgh
Burgos
Burk
Burke
Burkett
Burkhart
Burkholder
Burks
Burleson
Burlingame
Burnet
Burnett
Burnham
Burns
Burnside
Burr
Burrell
Burris
Burroughs
Burrows
Burt
Burton
Burwell
Busby
Busch
Bush
Bushnell

</td><td>

Buskirk
Bustamante
Butcher
Butler
Butt
Butterfield
Butterworth
Button
Butts
Buxton
Buzzard
Byers
Bynum
Byrd
Byrne
Byron
Caballero
Cable
Cabral
Cabrera
Cadwell
Cady
Cagle
Cahill
Cain
Calder
Calderon
Caldwell
Calhoun
Calkins
Callahan

</td></tr>
</table>

Callaway	Caroline
Calloway	Caron
Calvert	Carpenter
Calvin	Carr
Camacho	Carranza
Cameron	Carrasco
Camp	Carrico
Campbell	Carrier
Campbells	Carrillo
Campos	Carrington
Canady	Carroll
Canales	Carson
Canfield	Carter
Cannon	Cartwright
Cano	Caruso
Cantrell	Carver
Cantu	Cary
Capen	Case
Capps	Casey
Card	Cash
Cardenas	Casillas
Cardona	Cason
Carey	Cass
Carlisle	Cassel
Carlson	Cassidy
Carlton	Castaneda
Carman	Castellanos
Carmichael	Castillo
Carmona	Castle
Carnes	Castleberry
Carney	Castleman

Castro
Caswell
Cates
Catherine
Cathey
Catholic
Catlin
Caudill
Caudle
Cavanaugh
Cave
Cavendish
Cervantes
Chacon
Chaffee
Chaffin
Chalmers
Chamberlain
Chamberland
Chamberlin
Chambers
Champagne
Champion
Champlin
Chan
Chance
Chandler
Chaney
Chang
Chante
Chapin

Chaplin
Chapman
Chappell
Charles
Charlton
Chase
Chasse
Chatfield
Chatman
Chavez
Chaworth
Cheek
Cheever
Chen
Cheney
Cheng
Chenoweth
Cherry
Chesebrough
Chestnut
Chew
Child
Childers
Children
Childress
Childs
Chilton
Chin
Chipman
Chisholm
Chittenden

Chitwood
Cho
Choate
Choi
Christ
Christensen
Christian
Christiansen
Christie
Christopher
Christy
Chu
Chung
Church
Churchill
Cisneros
City
Clair
Clap
Clapp
Clare
Clark
Clarke
Clarkson
Clary
Clawson
Clay
Clayton
Clemens
Clement
Clements

Clemons
Clerk
Cleveland
Clevenger
Clifford
Clifton
Cline
Clinton
Close
Cloud
Cloutier
Co
Coates
Coats
Cobb
Coble
Coburn
Cochran
Cochrane
Cock
Cocke
Cockrell
Cody
Coe
Coffee
Coffey
Coffin
Coffman
Coggeshall
Cohen
Coker

Colbert
Colburn
Colby
Cole
Colegrove
Coleman
College
Collier
Collins
Colon
Colson
Colton
Colvin
Colwell
Combs
Comer
Compton
Comstock
Comyn
Conant
Cone
Conklin
Conkling
Conley
Conn
Connell
Connelly
Conner
Connolly
Connor
Connors

Conrad
Constable
Contreras
Converse
Conway
Conyers
Cook
Cooke
Cooley
Coolidge
Coombs
Coon
Coons
Cooper
Cope
Copeland
Copley
Corbett
Corbin
Corcoran
Cordell
Cordero
Cordova
Corey
Corley
Cormier
Corn
Cornelius
Cornell
Cornett
Cornish

Cornwall
Cornwell
Corona
Coronado
Correa
Correspondence
Corson
Cortes
Cortez
Corwin
Cory
Cosby
Costa
Costello
Costner
Cote
Cottle
Cotton
Cottrell
Couch
Coulter
Counts
County
Courtenay
Courtney
Cousins
Covell
Covert
Covey
Covington
Cowan

Cowden
Cowell
Cowles
Cox
Coy
Coyle
Coyne
Crabb
Crabtree
Craft
Crafts
Craig
Crain
Cram
Cramer
Crandall
Crane
Crank
Craven
Crawford
Creech
Creel
Crenshaw
Crews
Crider
Crisp
Crites
Crittenden
Crocker
Crockett
Croft

Cronin	Curtis
Crook	Curtiss
Crooks	Cushing
Crosby	Cushman
Crosley	Custer
Cross	Cutler
Croteau	Cutright
Crouch	Cutter
Crouse	Cutting
Crow	Cyr
Crowder	Dahl
Crowe	Daigle
Crowell	Dailey
Crowley	Daily
Crum	Dale
Crump	Daley
Cruz	Dallas
Cuellar	Dalrymple
Cuevas	Dalton
Culbertson	Daly
Cullen	Damon
Culp	Dana
Culpepper	Dane
Culver	Dang
Cummings	Daniel
Cummins	Daniels
Cunningham	Danielson
Cupp	Darby
Curran	Darcy
Currie	Darling
Curry	Darnell

Darrow
Daugherty
Daughter
Davenport
Davey
David
Davidson
Davies
Davila
Davis
Davison
Davisson
Dawes
Dawson
Day
Dayton
Deacon
Deal
Dean
Deane
Dearborn
Deaton
Deaver
Debord
Dec
Decker
Dehart
Dejesus
Delacruz
Delaney
Delarosa

Delatorre
Deleon
Delgado
Deloach
Delong
Delpeche
Demarest
Dempsey
Denham
Denison
Denney
Dennis
Dennison
Denny
Dent
Denton
Derby
Despencer
Despenser
Devereux
Devine
Devore
Deweese
Dewey
Dewitt
Dexter
Deyo
Diamond
Diaz
Dibble
Dice

Dick
Dickens
Dickenson
Dickerman
Dickerson
Dickey
Dickinson
Dickson
Diehl
Dietz
Dill
Dillard
Dillingham
Dillon
Dix
Dixon
Dizzly
Do
Doan
Dobbins
Dobbs
Dobson
Dockery
Dodd
Dodds
Dodge
Dodson
Doggett
Doherty
Dolan
Dole

Dominguez
Donahue
Donald
Donaldson
Donnelly
Donovan
Dooley
Doolittle
Dorman
Dorr
Dorsey
Doss
Dotson
Doty
Dougherty
Doughty
Douglas
Douglass
Dove
Dow
Dowden
Dowell
Dowling
Downer
Downey
Downing
Downs
Doyle
Doyley
Drake
Draper

Dresser
Drew
Driscoll
Driver
Drum
Drummett
Drummond
Drury
Dryden
Duarte
Dube
Duber
Duberry
Dubois
Dubose
Duchess
Dudley
Duff
Duffield
Duffy
Dugan
Dugger
Duke
Dukes
Dumas
Dumont
Dunbar
Duncan
Dungan
Dunham
Dunlap

Dunn
Dunning
Dunton
Duong
Dupree
Duran
Durand
Durant
Durbin
Durfee
Durham
Durkee
Dusseck
Dutton
Duval
Duvall
Dwyer
Dye
Dyer
Dyke
Dykes
Dypree
Eads
Earl
Early
Earnest
Earp
Easley
Eason
East
Easterly

Eastman
Easton
Eaton
Eby
Echols
Eck
Eckert
Ecosse
Eddy
Edelen
Edgar
Edge
Edgerton
Edgington
Edmonds
Edmondson
Edmunds
Edson
Edward
Edwards
Edwin
Eells
Egan
Egerton
Eggleston
Elam
Elder
Eldred
Eldredge
Eldridge
Elias
Eliza
Elizabeth
Elkins
Ellen
Eller
Elliot
Elliott
Ellis
Ellison
Elmer
Elmore
Elrod
Elwell
Ely
Embry
Emerson
Emery
Emily
Emma
Endicott
Engel
England
Engle
English
Ennis
Enriquez
Ensminger
Epperson
Epps
Erb
Erickson

Ernst
Erskine
Ervin
Erwin
Escobar
Escobedo
Esparza
Espinosa
Espinoza
Esposito
Esq
Esquivel
Estep
Estes
Estrada
Etheridge
Etten
Eubanks
Eugene
Evans
Eveleigh
Everett
Everhart
Ewing
Eyre
Ezell
Fagan
Fain
Fair
Fairbank
Fairbanks

Fairchild
Fanning
Farley
Farmer
Farnham
Farnum
Farr
Farrar
Farrell
Farrington
Farris
Farrow
Farthing
Farwell
Faulkner
Fay
Feb
Feldman
Feliciano
Felix
Fell
Fellows
Felt
Felton
Fenn
Fenner
Fenton
Ferguson
Fernandez
Ferreira
Ferrell

Ferrers
Ferris
Fessenden
Field
Fields
Fiennes
Fife
Fifield
Figueroa
Finch
Findley
Fine
Fink
Finley
Finn
Finney
Fischer
Fish
Fisher
Fiske
Fitch
Fite
Fitz
Fitzalan
Fitzgerald
Fitzhugh
Fitzpatrick
Fitzwilliam
Flaherty
Flanagan
Flanders

Fleming
Fletcher
Flinn
Flint
Flood
Flora
Florence
Flores
Flory
Flower
Flowers
Floyd
Fluellen
Flynn
Fogg
Foley
Folger
Folsom
Fonseca
Fontaine
Fontenot
Foor
Foote
Forbes
Ford
Fordham
Foreman
Forest
Forman
Forney
Forrest

Forrester
Forster
Forsyth
Fort
Fortin
Fortner
Foshee
Foss
Foster
Fountain
Fournier
Foust
Fouts
Fowle
Fowler
Fox
Fozzard
Frame
France
Frances
Francis
Francisco
Franco
Frank
Franklin
Franks
Frantz
Fraser
Frazer
Frazier
Frechette

Frederick
Freed
Freeland
Freeman
French
Fretz
Frey
Friedman
Friend
Fritz
Frost
Fry
Frye
Fuentes
Fugate
Fuller
Fullerton
Fulton
Funk
Furr
Futch
Gabbard
Gabriel
Gadberry
Gaddis
Gage
Gagne
Gagnon
Gaines
Gaither
Galbraith

Gale
Galindo
Gallagher
Gallardo
Gallegos
Gallo
Galloway
Gallup
Galpin
Galvan
Gamble
Gamez
Gann
Gant
Garber
Garcia
Gard
Gardiner
Gardner
Garfield
Garland
Garman
Garner
Garnes
Garnett
Garrett
Garrison
Garst
Garvin
Garwood
Gary
Garza
Gascoigne
Gaskill
Gassaway
Gaston
Gates
Gatlin
Gaunt
Gauthier
Gay
Geason
Gee
Geer
Geiger
Geneste
Gentry
George
Gerard
Gerber
Gerrish
Gertrude
Gervais
Gibbons
Gibbs
Gibson
Giddings
Giffard
Gifford
Gil
Gilbert
Gilbreath

Gilchrist	Godsey
Giles	Godwin
Gill	Goff
Gillenwaters	Goforth
Gillespie	Goins
Gillett	Gold
Gilliam	Goldberg
Gilliland	Golden
Gillis	Golding
Gilman	Goldman
Gilmer	Goldsmith
Gilmore	Goldstein
Gilpin	Gomes
Gilson	Gomez
Gilstrap	Gonzales
Ginger	Gooch
Giovanni	Good
Gipson	Goodale
Girard	Goode
Giroux	Goodenow
Givens	Goodman
Glasper	Goodnight
Glass	Goodrich
Gleason	Goodridge
Glen	Goodson
Glenn	Goodwin
Glover	Goosy
Goad	Gordan
Goble	Gordon
Goddard	Gore
Godfrey	Gorham

Gorman
Gorton
Goss
Gossett
Gough
Gould
Gove
Grace
Grady
Graff
Graham
Granados
Granger
Grant
Grantham
Graves
Gray
Graybeal
Grayson
Greco
Greeley
Green
Greenberg
Greene
Greenfield
Greenleaf
Greenlee
Greenwood
Greer
Gregg
Gregory

Gresham
Grey
Gridley
Griffin
Griffith
Griffiths
Griggs
Grigsby
Grimes
Grimm
Grinnell
Griswold
Groff
Gross
Grossman
Grosvenor
Grove
Grover
Groves
Grubbs
Guerra
Guerrero
Guest
Guevara
Guidry
Guild
Guillen
Guillot
Guinn
Gulick
Gunn

Gunter
Gunville
Gurney
Gushing
Gustafson
Gustin
Guthrie
Gutierrez
Guy
Guyton
Guzman
Haas
Hackett
Hackney
Hadley
Hagan
Hagen
Hager
Haggard
Hahn
Haight
Haines
Halbert
Hale
Hales
Haley
Hall
Hallett
Hallman
Hallmark
Hallock

Halsey
Halstead
Ham
Hamblin
Hamby
Hamilton
Hamlin
Hamm
Hammer
Hammond
Hampton
Hamrick
Han
Hancock
Hand
Handley
Handy
Haney
Hankerson
Hankins
Hanks
Hanley
Hanna
Hannah
Hansen
Hanson
Hara
Harbaugh
Harden
Hardesty
Hardin

Harding
Hardison
Hardman
Hardwick
Hardy
Hare
Hargrove
Harlan
Harley
Harlow
Harman
Harmon
Harper
Harps
Harrell
Harriman
Harrington
Harris
Harrison
Harrold
Harry
Harshman
Hart
Harter
Hartley
Hartman
Hartwell
Harvey
Hash
Haskell
Haskins

Hastings
Hatch
Hatchard
Hatcher
Hatfield
Hathaway
Hatton
Hauser
Haven
Havens
Hawk
Hawkes
Hawkins
Hawks
Hawley
Haworth
Hawthorne
Hay
Hayden
Hayes
Haynes
Hays
Hayward
Haywood
Hazard
Hazen
He
Head
Headley
Healey
Healy

Heard

Hearn

Heart

Heath

Heaton

Hebert

Heck

Hedrick

Heel

Heflin

Helen

Heller

Helm

Helms

Helton

Hemenway

Hemphill

Henderson

Hendrick

Hendricks

Hendrickson

Hendrix

Henley

Henry

Henshaw

Hensley

Henson

Hepburn

Herbert

Herman

Hernandez

Herndon

Herr

Herrera

Herrick

Herring

Herrington

Herron

Hersey

Hershberger

Hess

Hester

Heureux

Hewes

Hewett

Hewitt

Heywood

Hibbard

Hickey

Hickman

Hicks

Hidalgo

Higbee

Higby

Higdon

Higgins

High

Hightower

Higley

Hildebrand

Hildreth

Hill

Hilliard
Hillman
Hills
Hilton
Hinckley
Hinds
Hines
Hinkle
Hinman
Hinojosa
Hinshaw
Hinson
Hinton
Hirsch
Hitchcock
Hite
Hitt
Hixson
Ho
Hoang
Hoar
Hobart
Hobbs
Hochstetler
Hodge
Hodges
Hodgson
Hoey
Hoff
Hoffman
Hogan

Hoge
Hogg
Hogue
Holand
Holbrook
Holcomb
Holden
Holder
Holeman
Holland
Holley
Holliday
Hollingsworth
Hollis
Hollister
Holloway
Holly
Holman
Holmes
Holt
Holton
Home
Homer
Honeycutt
Hong
Hood
Hooker
Hooper
Hoover
Hope
Hopkins

Hopper	Hubbell
Horn	Hubbs
Hornbeck	Huber
Horne	Huddleston
Horner	Hudgins
Horton	Hudnall
Hoskins	Hudson
Hosmer	Huerta
Hospital	Huff
Hostetler	Huffman
Hostetter	Hufford
Hotchkiss	Huggins
Houck	Hughes
Hough	Hull
Houghton	Hume
House	Hummel
Houser	Humphrey
Houston	Humphreys
Houten	Humphries
Hovey	Hungerford
Howard	Hunt
Howe	Hunter
Howell	Huntington
Howes	Huntley
Howland	Hurd
Howlett	Hurlburt
Hoy	Hurlbut
Hoyle	Hurley
Hoyt	Hurst
Huang	Hurt
Hubbard	Hurtado

Hussey	Ivey
Huston	Jack
Hutchings	Jackman
Hutchins	Jackson
Hutchinson	Jacob
Hutchison	Jacobs
Hutson	Jacobsen
Hutton	Jacobson
Huynh	Jacques
Hyatt	James
Hyde	Jameson
Ibarra	Jamison
Ice	Jan
Ingalls	Jane
Ingersoll	Janes
Ingraham	Jansen
Ingram	Jaramillo
Inman	Jarrell
Innes	Jarrett
Irby	Jarvis
Ireland	Jay
Irish	Jean
Irvin	Jean-Pierre
Irvine	Jeffers
Irving	Jefferson
Irwin	Jeffrey
Isaac	Jeffries
Isaacs	Jenkins
Isbell	Jenks
Isham	Jennings
Island	Jensen

Jernigan
Jessee
Jessup
Jester
Jewell
Jewett
Jimenez
John
Johns
Johnson
Johnston
Johnstone
Joiner
Jolley
Jolly
Jones
Jordan
Jorgensen
Joseph
Josephine
Joslin
Joyce
Joyner
Juarez
Judd
Judkins
Judson
Judy
Julian
Jung
Justice

Kaiser
Kane
Kang
Kaplan
Katz
Kauffman
Kaufman
Kaur
Kay
Kearney
Keck
Keefe
Keeler
Keen
Keenan
Keene
Keeney
Keesee
Keffer
Keim
Keith
Keller
Kelley
Kellogg
Kelly
Kelso
Kemp
Kemper
Kendall
Kendrick
Kennedy

Kenney
Kenny
Kent
Ker
Kern
Kerns
Kerr
Kessler
Ketcham
Ketchum
Key
Keyes
Keys
Keyser
Khan
Kidd
Kidder
Kilby
Kilgore
Killian
Killough
Kilpatrick
Kim
Kimball
Kimble
Kimbrough
Kincaid
Kinder
King
Kingman
Kingsley
Kinney
Kinsey
Kirby
Kirk
Kirkham
Kirkland
Kirkman
Kirkpatrick
Kiser
Kistler
Kitchen
Kivett
Klein
Kline
Knapp
Kneeland
Knight
Knott
Knowles
Knox
Koch
Koehler
Koenig
Kolb
Kole
Koontz
Kowalski
Kraft
Kramer
Kraus
Krause

Krueger	Langford
Kruse	Langley
Kuhn	Langlois
Kurtz	Langston
Kutto	Lanham
Kuykendall	Lanier
Kyle	Lantz
Lacey	Lara
Lackey	Large
Lacy	Larkin
Ladd	Larkins
Laird	Larsen
Lake	Larson
Lam	Larue
Lamb	Lassiter
Lambert	Last Name
Lampkin	Latham
Lamson	Lathrop
Lancaster	Latimer
Lance	Latta
Land	Lau
Landers	Laughlin
Landis	Law
Landon	Lawler
Landrum	Lawrence
Landry	Laws
Lane	Lawson
Laney	Lawton
Lang	Lay
Langdon	Layman
Lange	Layton

Le
Lea
Leach
Leal
Learned
Leary
Leatherman
Leavenworth
Leavitt
Leblanc
Ledbetter
Ledford
Lee
Leech
Leeds
Lees
Leete
Lefebvre
Leger
Leggett
Lehigh
Lehman
Leigh
Leighton
Leland
Lemaster
Lemay
Lemire
Lemon
Lemyre
Lennon
Lentz
Leon
Leonard
Leroy
Leslie
Lessard
Lester
Leung
Levesque
Levin
Levine
Levy
Lewis
Leyva
Li
Light
Lightfoot
Lillie
Lilly
Lim
Lin
Lincoln
Linder
Lindley
Lindsay
Lindsey
Link
Linn
Linton
Lippincott
Lister

Litchfield
Litchmore
Little
Littlefield
Littleton
Liu
Lively
Living
Livingston
Lloyd
Lnu
Lock
Locke
Locket
Lockhart
Locklear
Lockwood
Lodge
Logan
Logsdon
Lombard
London
Long
Longley
Loomis
Looney
Looper
Lopez
Lord
Lorraine
Lothrop

Lott
Louis
Louisa
Louise
Love
Lovejoy
Lovelace
Loveland
Loveless
Lovell
Lovett
Low
Lowe
Lowell
Lowery
Lowry
Lowther
Loy
Loyd
Lozano
Lu
Lucas
Luce
Lucero
Lucket
Lucy
Ludlow
Ludwig
Lugo
Lujan
Luke

Lukes
Luna
Lund
Lundy
Lunsford
Lunt
Lusk
Luther
Luttrell
Lutz
Lyle
Lyman
Lynch
Lynde
Lyndsy
Lynn
Lyon
Lyons
Lytle
Mabry
Macdonald
Mace
Machado
Macias
Mack
Mackay
Mackenzie
Mackey
Maclean
Macleod
Macomber

Macy
Madden
Maddox
Madison
Madrid
Madrigal
Maeyo
Magana
Magee
Mahan
Maher
Mahoney
Main
Mainwaring
Major
Malcolm
Maldonado
Mallory
Malone
Maloney
Man
Manchester
Mandeville
Manley
Mann
Manning
Mansfield
Manuel
Mapes
Maples
Mar

Marble
March
Marcum
Marcus
Marcy
Margaret
Maria
Marie
Mariee
Marin
Marino
Markham
Markley
Marks
Marley
Marlow
Marquez
Marr
Marrero
Marsh
Marshal
Marshall
Marsolais
Martel
Martha
Martin
Martinez
Martyn
Marvel
Marvin
Mary

Mason
Massey
Massie
Mast
Masters
Masterson
Mata
Matheny
Mathew
Mathews
Mathewson
Mathis
Matilda
Matlock
Matos
Matson
Matteson
Matthews
Mauldin
Maupin
Maurer
Maxey
Maxson
Maxwell
May
Mayberry
Mayer
Mayes
Mayfield
Maynard
Mayo

Mays
Mc Cain
Mc Cane
Mc Clinton
Mc Clousky
Mc Coy
Mc Cray
Mc Donald
Mc Gill
Mc Grew
Mc Kinnon
Mcadams
Mcallister
Mcarthur
Mcbride
Mccabe
Mccain
Mccall
Mccallum
Mccann
Mccarthy
Mccartney
Mccarty
Mccauley
Mcclain
Mcclellan
Mcclelland
Mcclendon
Mcclung
Mcclure
Mccollum

Mcconnell
Mccord
Mccormack
Mccormick
Mccoy
Mccracken
Mccray
Mcculloch
Mccullough
Mccune
Mccurdy
Mcdaniel
Mcdermott
Mcdonald
Mcdonough
Mcdowell
Mcelroy
Mcfadden
Mcfarland
Mcgee
Mcgehee
Mcghee
Mcgill
Mcginnis
Mcgovern
Mcgowan
Mcgrath
Mcgraw
Mcgregor
Mcgrew
Mcguire

Mchugh	Mcwhorter
Mcintire	Mcwilliams
Mcintosh	Meacham
Mcintyre	Mead
Mckay	Meade
Mckee	Meador
Mckenna	Meadows
Mckenzie	Means
Mckinley	Mears
Mckinney	Medeiros
Mcknight	Medger
Mclain	Medina
Mclaughlin	Medley
Mclean	Medrano
Mcleod	Meek
Mcmahan	Meeker
Mcmahon	Meeks
Mcmanus	Meier
Mcmillan	Meigs
Mcmullen	Mejia
Mcnabb	Melancon
Mcnair	Melendez
Mcnamara	Mellott
Mcneal	Melton
Mcneil	Melville
Mcneill	Melvin
Mcnutt	Menard
Mcpherson	Mendenhall
Mcqueen	Mendez
Mcrae	Mendoza
Mcvey	Mentioned

Mercado

Mercer

Merchant

Mercia

Meredith

Merrell

Merriam

Merrill

Merriman

Merritt

Merry

Meschines

Messenger

Messer

Metcalf

Meter

Metz

Metzger

Meyer

Meyers

Meza

Michael

Michaels

Michaud

Michel

Middleton

Milam

Milburn

Miles

Millar

Millard

Miller

Milligan

Milliken

Milliron

Mills

Milne

Milner

Milton

Mim

Mims

Mincey

Miner

Minor

Minot

Minter

Minton

Miracle

Miranda

Mitchel

Mitchell

Mitchells

Mixon

Mize

Mobley

Mock

Moffett

Mohr

Molina

Molyneux

Monk

Monroe

Montagu
Montague
Montalvo
Montana
Montano
Montes
Montfort
Montgomery
Montoya
Moody
Moon
Mooney
Moore
Moorman
Mora
Morales
Moran
Morehead
Morehouse
Moreland
Moreno
Morey
Morgan
Morin
Morissette
Morley
Morrell
Morris
Morrison
Morrow
Morse

Mortimer
Morton
Moseley
Moser
Moses
Mosher
Mosley
Moss
Mott
Moulton
Mount
Mowbray
Mowry
Moyer
Mudd
Mudge
Mueller
Muhammad
Muir
Mulford
Mullen
Mullens
Muller
Mullican
Mullinax
Mullins
Mumford
Munger
Muniz
Munn
Munoz

Munro
Munroe
Munsell
Munson
Murdock
Murillo
Murphree
Murphy
Murray
Murrell
Musgrave
Musick
Musser
Myers
Myrick
Nance
Nancy
Napier
Nash
Nason
Nation
Nava
Navarre
Navarro
Nay
Naylor
Neal
Neale
Needham
Neel
Neeley

Neely
Neff
Neill
Nelson
Ness
Nettleton
Neumann
Nevill
Neville
New
Newberry
Newby
Newcomer
Newell
Newkirk
Newland
Newlin
Newman
Newsom
Newsome
Newton
Nguyen
Nicholas
Nicholls
Nichols
Nicholson
Nickerson
Nickolson
Nielsen
Nieto
Nieves

Niles	Oates
Nix	Obrien
Nixon	Ocampo
Noble	Ochoa
Noe	Oconnell
Noel	Oconnor
Nolan	Odell
Noland	Odom
Nolen	Odonnell
Norfleet	Ogden
Norman	Ogilvie
Normandie	Ohara
Norris	Okeefe
North	Oleary
Northrup	Oliphant
Norton	Olivares
Norwood	Oliver
Nott	Olmstead
Nottingham	Olmsted
Novak	Olney
Nowak	Olsen
Noyes	Olson
Nugent	Olvera
Nunez	Omalley
Nunn	Oneal
Nutt	Oneil
Nutter	Oneill
Nutting	Orcutt
Nye	Ornelas
Oakes	Orozco
Oakley	Ortega

Ortiz
Osborn
Osborne
Osbourne
Osgood
Osorio
Ostrander
Oswald
Otero
Otis
Otto
Overman
Overton
Owen
Owens
Oxford
O'conner
O'waller
Pace
Pacheco
Pack
Packard
Packer
Paddock
Padgett
Padilla
Pagan
Page
Paige
Paine
Painter

Palacios
Palmer
Pappas
Pare
Paredes
Parent
Paris
Parish
Park
Parke
Parker
Parkinson
Parks
Parmenter
Parnell
Parr
Parra
Parris
Parrish
Parrott
Parry
Parsons
Partridge
Pass
Patch
Pate
Patel
Patrick
Pattenden
Patterson
Patton

Paul
Pauley
Paulson
Paxton
Payne
Payson
Payton
Paz
Peabody
Peacock
Peak
Peake
Peaks
Pearce
Pearl
Pearsall
Pearson
Pease
Peavey
Peck
Peckham
Pedersen
Pedigo
Peebles
Peek
Peel
Peirce
Pelham
Pelletier
Pelton
Pemberton

Pena
Pence
Pendleton
Penn
Pennell
Pennington
Penny
Pentecost
Peoples
Pepper
Peralta
Percy
Perdue
Pereira
Perez
Perkins
Perrin
Perry
Person
Peter
Peterman
Peters
Petersen
Peterson
Pettit
Petty
Peyton
Pham
Phan
Phelps
Philbrick

Philip
Philips
Phillips
Phinney
Phipps
Piatt
Pickard
Pickens
Pickering
Pickett
Pierce
Pierre
Pierson
Pike
Pina
Pineda
Pinkerton
Pinkham
Pinkney
Pinney
Pinson
Pinto
Piper
Pitcher
Pitman
Pits
Pitt
Pittard
Pittman
Pitts
Place

Plantagenet
Platt
Plumb
Plummer
Plunkett
Poe
Poindexter
Poirier
Poland
Pole
Poling
Polk
Pollard
Pollock
Polly
Pomeroy
Ponce
Pool
Poole
Poor
Poore
Pope
Porter
Portillo
Posey
Post
Poston
Potter
Potts
Pough
Powell

Power
Powers
Prado
Prater
Prather
Pratt
Pray
Prence
Prentiss
Prescott
Presley
Preston
Prewitt
Price
Prichard
Prince
Pringle
Prior
Pritchard
Pritchett
Private
Procter
Proctor
Proffitt
Prouty
Provost
Pruett
Pruitt
Pryor
Puckett
Pugh

Purcell
Purnsley
Purvis
Puterbaugh
Putman
Putnam
Pyle
Qualls
Queen
Quezada
Quick
Quigley
Quimby
Quinby
Quinn
Quinones
Quintana
Quintero
Quiroz
Radcliffe
Rader
Radford
Ragsdale
Raines
Rainey
Rains
Ralph
Ralston
Rambo
Ramey
Ramirez

Ramos
Ramsay
Ramsey
Randall
Randolph
Rangel
Rankin
Ransom
Rasmussen
Rathbone
Rathbun
Ratliff
Rawlings
Rawlins
Ray
Raymond
Read
Reade
Reagan
Reaves
Rebecca
Reber
Records
Rector
Reddick
Redding
Redman
Redmond
Reece
Reed
Reeder

Reedy
Rees
Reese
Reeve
Reeves
Regan
Register
Reid
Reilly
Remington
Renteria
Reyes
Reyna
Reynolds
Rhea
Rhoades
Rhoads
Rhodes
Rhyne
Rice
Rich
Richard
Richards
Richardson
Richey
Richmond
Richter
Rickard
Ricker
Ricketts
Ricks

Rico
Riddell
Riddle
Ridenour
Rider
Ridgeway
Ridley
Riffle
Riggs
Riley
Rinehart
Ring
Rios
Risley
Ritchey
Ritchie
Ritter
Rivas
River
Rivera
Rivers
Rives
Rizzo
Roach
Roark
Robb
Robbins
Robe
Roberson
Robert
Roberts

Robertson
Robinett
Robinette
Robins
Robinson
Robison
Robles
Robson
Roby
Rocha
Roche
Rochester
Rock
Rockwood
Rodgers
Rodman
Rodrigues
Rodriguez
Rodriquez
Roe
Rogers
Rojas
Roland
Rolfe
Roller
Rollins
Rolon
Roman
Romano
Romero
Romine

Romo
Roosa
Roosevelt
Root
Roper
Ros
Rosa
Rosado
Rosales
Rosario
Rosas
Rose
Rosen
Rosenberg
Rosenberger
Rosenthal
Ross
Rosser
Rossi
Roth
Rothgeb
Rouse
Roush
Rowan
Rowe
Rowell
Rowland
Rowley
Roy
Royal
Royce

Royer
Rubin
Rubio
Ruble
Rucker
Rudd
Rudolph
Ruff
Ruggles
Ruiz
Rumsey
Rupp
Rush
Rushing
Rushton
Russ
Russel
Russell
Russo
Rust
Ruth
Rutherford
Rutledge
Rutter
Ryan
Ryder
Sackett
Sadler
Saenz
Sage
Sager

Salas
Salazar
Saldana
Salgado
Salinas
Salisbury
Salls
Salmon
Salter
Sample
Sampson
Sams
Samson
Samuel
Samuels
Sanborn
Sanchez
Sanders
Sanderson
Sandford
Sandord
Sandoval
Sands
Sanford
Santana
Santiago
Santos
Sapp
Sarah
Sargent
Satterfield

Saucedo
Saunders
Savage
Sawyer
Saxton
Saye
Sayers
Sayles
Saylor
Sayre
Scales
Scarborough
Schaefer
Schaeffer
Schafer
Schaffer
Schell
Schenck
Schilling
Schmidt
Schmitt
Schmitz
Schneider
Schofield
Schoonmaker
Schroeder
Schultz
Schulz
Schumacher
Schuster
Schuyler

Schwab
Schwartz
Scofield
Scotia
Scotland
Scott
Scribner
Scrope
Scruggs
Scudder
Seale
Seaman
Searle
Sears
Seaton
Seavey
Seay
Secord
Sedgwick
Seebran
Seeley
Segrave
Segura
Selby
Selden
Sellers
Sells
Sept
Serna
Serrano
Sessions

Seton
Sevier
Sewall
Seward
Sewell
Sexton
Seymour
Shackelford
Shafer
Shaffer
Shah
Shank
Shanks
Shannon
Shapiro
Sharp
Sharpe
Shattuck
Shaver
Shaw
Shea
Shearer
Shearin
Sheehan
Sheets
Sheffield
Shelby
Sheldon
Shell
Shelley
Shelton

Shepard
Shepherd
Sheppard
Sherburne
Sheridan
Sherman
Sherwood
Shields
Shinn
Shipley
Shipp
Shirk
Shirley
Shoaf
Shockley
Shoemaker
Shook
Short
Showalter
Shreve
Shuey
Shugart
Shultz
Shumway
Sibley
Siegel
Sierra
Sigler
Sikes
Siler
Silva

Silver
Simmons
Simms
Simon
Simone
Simons
Simpson
Sims
Sinclair
Singer
Singh
Singleton
Sink
Sisco
Sisk
Sisson
Sizemore
Skaggs
Skidmore
Skillman
Skinner
Slack
Slade
Slater
Slaton
Slaughter
Slayton
Sloan
Slocum
Small
Smalley

Smalls	Southwick
Smallwood	Souza
Smart	Sowers
Smedley	Spalding
Smiley	Spang
Smith	Spangler
Smithson	Sparhawk
Smoot	Sparkman
Smyth	Sparks
Smythe	Sparrow
Snavely	Spaulding
Sneed	Spear
Snell	Spears
Snider	Speck
Snodgrass	Speed
Snow	Speer
Snyder	Spence
Solano	Spencer
Solis	Sperry
Solomon	Spicer
Somers	Spiller
Song	Spivey
Soper	Spooner
Sophia	Sprague
Sorensen	Spring
Soriano	Springer
Sosa	Springs
Soto	Sprinkle
Soule	Spruwill
South	Spurgeon
Southard	Spurlock

Squire
Squires
Stacey
Stacy
Stafford
Stagg
Stahl
Staley
Stallard
Stallings
Stalnaker
Stamper
Standford
Standish
Standley
Stanfield
Stanford
Stanley
Stanton
Stapleton
Stapp
Starbuck
Stark
Starkey
Starks
Starling
Starnes
Starr
Stauffer
Stearns
Stebbins

Stedman
Steele
Stein
Steiner
Stenson
Stephen
Stephens
Stephenson
Stepp
Sterling
Stern
Stetson
Stevens
Stevenson
Steward
Stewart
Stickney
Stiles
Still
Stillman
Stillwell
Stinson
Stirling
Stites
Stocker
Stockett
Stockton
Stockwell
Stoddard
Stokes
Stone

Storey	Sturtevant
Story	Styles
Stoughton	Suarez
Stourton	Sullins
Stout	Sullivan
Stovall	Sultan
Stover	Summers
Stow	Sumner
Stowe	Susan
Stowell	Sutherland
Strange	Sutton
Stratton	Swain
Strawn	Swan
Street	Swann
Streeter	Swanson
Strickland	Swartwout
Strickler	Swartz
Stringer	Swearingen
Strode	Sweeney
Strong	Sweet
Strother	Swenson
Stroud	Swett
Stroup	Swift
Struble	Swisher
Strunk	Switzer
Stuart	Swope
Stubblefield	Sykes
Stubbs	Sylvester
Stump	Syme
Sturgis	Symmes
Sturm	Symonds

Taber
Tabor
Tackett
Taggart
Talbot
Talbott
Talcott
Taliaferro
Talley
Tallman
Tang
Tanner
Tapia
Tarbell
Tate
Tatum
Taylor
Teague
Tempest
Temple
Templeton
Tennant
Tenney
Terrell
Terrill
Terry
Thacher
Thacker
Tharp
Thatcher
Thayer

Thibaudeau
Thibodeau
Thomas
Thomason
Thomasson
Thompson
Thomson
Thorne
Thornton
Thorp
Thorpe
Thrasher
Thurman
Thurston
Tibbetts
Tidd
Tidwell
Tiffany
Till
Tilley
Tillman
Tillotson
Tilson
Tilston
Tilton
Timmons
Tingley
Tinker
Tinkham
Tinsley
Tipton

Tisdale
Tison
Titsworth
Titus
Tobey
Tobias
Tobin
Todd
Toddart
Tolbert
Tolman
Tomes
Tomlinson
Tompkins
Toney
Toole
Torres
Torrey
Toth
Totten
Tovar
Tower
Towle
Town
Towne
Townley
Townsend
Township
Tracy
Trahan
Trammell

Tran
Trask
Travis
Treadway
Treadwell
Treat
Trejo
Tremblay
Trent
Trevino
Trimble
Triplett
Tripp
Troops
Trotter
Trounce
Trout
Trowbridge
Troxell
Truax
True
Trueblood
Truesdell
Truitt
Trujillo
Truman
Trumbull
Truong
Tryon
Tubbs
Tuck

Tucker
Tufts
Tupper
Turnbull
Turner
Turney
Turpin
Tuthill
Tuttle
Twitchell
Tyler
Tyson
Ulrich
Underhill
Underwood
Upham
Upton
Urban
Uribe
Usher
Utley
Valdez
Valencia
Valentine
Valenzuela
Valle
Vance
Vang
Varela
Vargas
Varner

Varney
Varnum
Vasquez
Vaughan
Vaughn
Vaught
Vaux
Vazquez
Vega
Vela
Velasco
Velasquez
Velazquez
Velez
Venable
Venables
Ventura
Vera
Vernon
Vest
Vestal
Vick
Vickers
Vickery
Vigil
Vilanni
Villa
Villegas
Vincent
Vinson
Vinton

Vogel
Voorhees
Vose
Voss
Vrooman
Waddell
Wade
Wadsworth
Waggoner
Wagner
Wagoner
Wait
Waite
Wake
Wakefield
Wakeman
Walden
Waldo
Waldron
Waldrop
Walker
Wall
Wallace
Waller
Walling
Wallis
Walls
Walpole
Walsh
Walter
Walters

Walton
Wampler
Wang
War
Ward
Warde
Warden
Ware
Warenne
Warfield
Waring
Warne
Warner
Warr
Warren
Warriner
Warth
Wash
Washburn
Washington
Wasson
Waterhouse
Waterman
Waters
Watkins
Watson
Watt
Watts
Waugh
Way
Wayne

Weab
Weatherby
Weatherford
Weaver
Webb
Webber
Weber
Webster
Weed
Weeden
Weekes
Weeks
Weir
Weiss
Welch
Weld
Weller
Welles
Wellington
Wellman
Wells
Welsh
Welton
Wendell
Wenger
Wentworth
Werling
Werner
Wertz
Wesley
Wessex

Wesson
West
Westbrook
Westcott
Westervelt
Westfall
Weston
Wetmore
Wetzel
Whalen
Whaley
Wharton
Whatley
Wheat
Wheatley
Wheaton
Wheeler
Whipple
Whit
Whitacre
Whitaker
Whitcomb
White
Whitehead
Whiteside
Whitfield
Whiting
Whitley
Whitlock
Whitman
Whitney

Whitson
Whitt
Whittaker
Whittemore
Whitten
Whittier
Whittington
Whitworth
Wickham
Wife
Wiggin
Wiggins
Wight
Wightman
Wilber
Wilbore
Wilbur
Wilcox
Wilcoxson
Wild
Wilde
Wilder
Wildman
Wiles
Wiley
Wilhelm
Wilhite
Wilkerson
Wilkes
Wilkins
Wilkinson

Will
Willard
Willett
Willey
William
Williams
Williamson
Willianson
Willingham
Willis
Wills
Wilmot
Wilson
Wilton
Winans
Winchester
Windsor
Wines
Wing
Wingate
Wingfield
Winkle
Winkler
Winn
Winns
Winship
Winslow
Winsor
Winstead
Winston
Winter

Winters
Winthrop
Wisdom
Wise
Wiseman
Withers
Withington
Withrow
Witt
Wofford
Wolf
Wolfe
Wolff
Womack
Wong
Wood
Woodall
Woodard
Woodbridge
Woodbury
Woodcock
Woodford
Woodly
Woodman
Woodruff
Woods
Woodward
Woody
Woolfolk
Woolley
Woolsey

Wooten
Worcester
Worden
Workman
Worley
Worth
Wray
Wren
Wright
Wyatt
Wyckoff
Wylie
Wyman
Wynn
Wynne
Wynter
Xiong
Yancey
Yanez
Yang
Yarbrough
Yates
Ybarra
Yeager
Yee
Yingling
Yocum
Yoder
York
Yost
Young

Youngblood
Younger
Youngs
Yount
Zachary
Zamora
Zapata
Zavala
Zepeda
Zhang
Ziegler
Zimmer
Zimmerman

WESTERN NAMES

Aaron
Abagail
Abbey
Abbie
Abbigail
Abby
Abigail
Abigale
Abigayle
Abraham
Ada
Adam
Addie
Addison
Adele
Adelle
Adina
Adrian
Adriana
Adrianna
Agatha
Agnes
Agnus
Aida
Aiden
Aimee
Aimes
Alan
Albert
Alberta
Alden
Alec
Alex
Alexa
Alexander
Alexandra
Alexandria
Alfalfa

<table>
<tr><td>Alfred</td><td>Annalisa</td></tr>
<tr><td>Alfreda</td><td>Annalise</td></tr>
<tr><td>Alice</td><td>Anne</td></tr>
<tr><td>Aliyah</td><td>Annie</td></tr>
<tr><td>Allan</td><td>Anson</td></tr>
<tr><td>Allen</td><td>Anthony</td></tr>
<tr><td>Allison</td><td>Antonio</td></tr>
<tr><td>Ally</td><td>Anya</td></tr>
<tr><td>Alondra</td><td>April</td></tr>
<tr><td>Alonzo</td><td>Arabella</td></tr>
<tr><td>Althea</td><td>Archy</td></tr>
<tr><td>Alton</td><td>Aria</td></tr>
<tr><td>Alyssa</td><td>Arianna</td></tr>
<tr><td>Amada</td><td>Arielle</td></tr>
<tr><td>Amalia</td><td>Arizona</td></tr>
<tr><td>Amanda</td><td>Arlington</td></tr>
<tr><td>Amber</td><td>Arlo</td></tr>
<tr><td>Ambrose</td><td>Armanda</td></tr>
<tr><td>Amelia</td><td>Art</td></tr>
<tr><td>Amie</td><td>Arthur</td></tr>
<tr><td>Amos</td><td>Asa</td></tr>
<tr><td>Amy</td><td>Asha</td></tr>
<tr><td>Anabel</td><td>Ashby</td></tr>
<tr><td>Anastasia</td><td>Asher</td></tr>
<tr><td>Andrew</td><td>Ashley</td></tr>
<tr><td>Andy</td><td>Ashly</td></tr>
<tr><td>Angelina</td><td>Ashton</td></tr>
<tr><td>Angeline</td><td>Asia</td></tr>
<tr><td>Anna</td><td>Aster</td></tr>
<tr><td>Annabell</td><td>Aubree</td></tr>
<tr><td>Annabelle</td><td>Aubrey</td></tr>
</table>

Auburn
Audie
Audrey
August
Augusta
Augustus
Aura
Aurelia
Aurora
Austin
Autumn
Ava
Avery
Axel
Azalea
Azure
Bailey
Bambi
Bao
Barb
Barbara
Barbie
Barclay
Bart
Basil
Bay
Baylee
Beatrice
Beau
Beck
Beckett

Becky
Bedford
Beige
Bella
Belle
Benjamin
Bennet
Bennett
Bentley
Benton
Berry
Bertha
Bertie
Bethanie
Betsy
Bette
Betty
Beverley
Beverly
Bianca
Bill/Billy
Billie
Billy
Birch
Birdie
Blair
Blaire
Blake
Blanch
Blanche
Blaze

Blossom
Blue
Bo
Bobbie
Bobbie-Sue
Bobby
Bolan
Bonney
Bonnie
Bonny
Boone
Borris
Boston
Boyd
Brandie
Brandon
Brandy
Brant
Brantley
Brantly
Brayden
Bree
Brenda
Brent
Bret
Brianna
Brice
Bridget
Bridgett
Bridgette
Brigitte

Britany
Britney
Brock
Brody
Brogan
Bronc
Bronco
Bronson
Brook
Brooklyn
Brooks
Brown
Bryce
Bryndle
Bryson
Buck
Buddy
Buffy
Bunny
Burgundy
Buster
Butch
Buzz
Cade
Caden
Cadence
Cage
Caid
Caitlin
Caitlyn
Cale

Caleb
Calla
Callie
Callum
Calvin
Camden
Cameron
Cami
Camilla
Cammie
Cammy
Camron
Canaan
Candace
Candis
Cane
Canyon
Cara
Carina
Carl
Carlos
Carlyle
Carmen
Carmine
Carol
Carolina
Caroline
Caroll
Carolynn
Carrie
Carrol

Carroll
Carry
Carson
Carter
Casandra
Casey
Cash
Cason
Cassandra
Cassey
Cassidy
Cassie
Cassius
Cassondra
Cassy
Catalina
Catharine
Catherine
Cathey
Cathy
Cayden
Cayla
Cecil
Cecilia
Cerise
Chad
Chance
Charity
Charleen
Charlene
Charles

Charlette	Cicely
Charley	Cindi
Charlie	Cindy
Charlotte	Cinn
Charlton	Claire
Charmaine	Clara
Chase	Clare
Chasidy	Clarence
Chasity	Clarice
Chassidy	Clark
Chauncey	Classie
Chaya	Claude
Chelsea	Claudette
Chelsey	Claudia
Chelsie	Claudine
Cherish	Clay
Cherry	Clayton
Cherryl	Clementine
Chesley	Cleo
Chet	Cletus
Cheyanne	Cliff
Cheyenne	Clifford
Chip	Clint
Chloe	Clinton
Chrissy	Clive
Christian	Clover
Christina	Clovis
Christine	Clyde
Christopher	Coby
Chuck	Codi
Ciara	Codie

Cody
Colby
Cole
Coleen
Coleman
Coletta
Colette
Colin
Colleen
Collen
Colt
Colton
Conner
Connie
Connor
Constance
Contessa
Coop
Cooper
Cora
Coral
Coralee
Corbin
Cord
Cordelia
Coreen
Corey
Corina
Cornelia
Cornelius
Corrie

Cortney
Cory
Cosette
Courtney
Coy
Craig
Crawford
Crissy
Crockett
Crystal
Cullen
Curt
Curtis
Cyan
Cynthia
Cyril
Cyrus
Dahlia
Daisey
Daisy
Dakota
Dale
Dallas
Dalton
Damon
Dan
Dana
Dane
Daniel
Dannie
Dante

Daphne
Daphnie
Darby
Darcey
Darleen
Darrell
Daryl
Dave
David
Dawn
Dawson
Dayson
Dean
Debbie
Debbra
Debby
Delancy
Delaney
Delilah
Dell
Delmar
Delores
Delphia
Delphine
Delta
Demetrius
Dempsey
Dena
Denese
Denise
Dennis
Denny
Denver
Deon
Deonna
Derby
Derringer
Desirae
Desire
Desiree
Despina
Dessie
Destry
Devin
Devon
Dexter
Dianna
Dianne
Dillard
Dion
Dirk
Dixie
Dixon
Dock
Dodie
Doliver
Dollie
Dolly
Dolores
Doloris
Dominic
Dominick

Donald	Edna
Donna	Edson
Donnie	Edward
Donovan	Edwin
Doreen	Edwina
Dori	Edyth
Dorthy	Effie
Dottie	Elanor
Dotty	Eldon
Dove	Eldridge
Doyle	Eleanor
Drake	Elenore
Drew	Eli
Drucilla	Elijah
Duke	Elisabeth
Dulcinea	Elise
Duncan	Eliza
Dustin	Elizabeth
Dusty	Ella
Dwayne	Ellen
Dwight	Ellena
Dylan	Ellie
Earl	Ellis
Easton	Elly
Eben	Elma
Ed	Elmer
Eddie	Elnora
Edelmira	Eloise
Eden	Eloy
Edgar	Elsa
Edith	Elsie

Elvira
Ember
Emerald
Emerson
Emilio
Emily
Emma
Emmett
Emogene
Emory
Enid
Eponine
Eric
Erica
Erin
Erlene
Eryn
Esmeralda
Esperanza
Essie
Estelle
Ester
Esther
Ethan
Ethel
Etta
Ettie
Eudora
Eugene
Eugenia
Eula

Eva
Evan
Evangelina
Evangeline
Eve
Evelyn
Everett
Evie
Evita
Ezrah
Fae
Fairy
Faith
Fannie
Fanny
Fantine
Farley
Faro
Farrah
Fawn
Fay
Faye
Felix
Fern
Finley
Fiona
Fiorello
Fletcher
Flint
Flo
Flora

Florance
Florence
Florida
Floyd
Flynn
Ford
Forest
Forrest
Foster
Fran
Frances
Francesca
Francine
Francis
Frank
Frankie
Fred
Freddie
Frederica
Freeda
Freeman
Freida
Fuchsia
Gabby
Gabe
Gabriel
Gabriella
Gabrielle
Gage
Gail
Gale

Galen
Galina
Gardner
Garland
Garnet
Garnett
Garrett
Garris
Garrison
Garth
Garvin
Gary
Gavin
Gearldine
Gema
Gemma
Gena
Gene
Geneva
Genie
Genny
Gentry
George
Georgeanna
Georgene
Georgette
Georgia
Georgianna
Georgianne
Georgie
Gerald

Geraldine
Gerdy
Gertie
Gertrude
Gia
Gianna
Gideon
Gigi
Gil
Gilberte
Gillian
Gina
Ginette
Ginger
Ginny
Giovanna
Giselle
Gladis
Glenda
Glenn
Glinda
Gloria
Glory
Goldie
Grace
Gracie
Grady
Graham
Grant
Grayson
Gregory

Greta
Gretchen
Gretta
Grey
Griffin
Grizabella
Guadalupe
Gus
Gussie
Gwen
Gwendolyn
Gwenn
Gwyn
Gwyneth
Gyn
Gypsy
Hadley
Hailee
Hailey
Hailie
Haley
Halle
Halley
Hallie
Hank
Hannah
Harlan
Harley
Harmony
Harold
Harper

Harriet	Hobart
Harriett	Holland
Harriette	Holley
Harrison	Hollie
Harry	Hollis
Harvey	Holly
Haskell	Honey
Hassie	Hope
Hattie	Horace
Haven	Houston
Hayden	Hoyt
Hayes	Huck
Hazel	Hudson
Heather	Hue
Hedy	Hugo
Heidi	Hunter
Heidy	Ian
Helen	Ida
Helene	Imogene
Helga	India
Hellen	Indigo
Henrietta	Inez
Henriette	Inga
Henry	Ingrid
Herman	Iona
Herschel	Irene
Hester	Iris
Hewitt	Isaac
Hilda	Isabel
Hildred	Isabell
Hillary	Isabella

Isabelle

Isadora

Isaiah

Israel

Ivan

Ivory

Ivy

Izabella

Jabe

Jace

Jack

Jackson

Jacob

Jade

Jaden

Jagger

Jaiden

Jaimee

Jaimie

Jake

James

Jamison

Jane

Janell

Janice

Jannette

Jarrett

Jarrod

Jarvis

Jasmine

Jason

Jasper

Jax

Jaxon

Jay

Jayda

Jayden

Jazmin

Jean

Jeb

Jed

Jefferson

Jeffrey

Jemma

Jen

Jenell

Jennie

Jenny

Jeraldine

Jeremiah

Jeremy

Jericho

Jerry

Jessamine

Jesse

Jessica

Jessie

Jet

Jethro

Jethroe

Jetro

Jetter

Jewel
Jill
Jillian
Jim
Jimbo
Jimmie
Jimmy
Jin
Jinny
Jo
Joan
Joanne
Jocelyn
Jock
Jodee
Jodi
Jodie
Jody
Joe
Joel
Joey
Johanna
Johanne
John
Johnny
Joi
Jon
Jonathan
Jone
Jordan
Jordyn

Josefina
Joseph
Josephina
Josephine
Josh
Joshua
Josiah
Josie
Journey
Jovan
Joy
Joya
Juan
Jude
Judith
Judson
Judy
Jule
Julia
Julian
Juliana
Julianna
Julianne
Julie
Juliet
June
Justice
Justin
Kaceton
Kacey
Kacie

Kacy
Kadence
Kaelyn
Kailey
Kaine
Kaitlin
Kaitlyn
Kal
Kala
Kaleah
Kallie
Kandace
Kandice
Karen
Karin
Karl
Karla
Karlee
Karley
Karlie
Karmen
Karrie
Karry
Kase
Kasey
Kate
Katelin
Katelyn
Katherine
Kathy
Katie

Katlyn
Katrice
Kattie
Kay
Kaydence
Kaylee
Kaylen
Keith
Kelley
Kelly
Kelsey
Kemberly
Ken
Kendal
Kendall
Kennedy
Kenneth
Kent
Kerri
Kerrie
Kerry
Kerstin
Kevin
Kierra
Kiersten
Kiley
Kim
Kimberly
Kinsey
Kirby
Kirsten

Kirstie

Kirstin

Kit

Knox

Kolt

Kortney

Kourtney

Kris

Krissy

Kristal

Kristen

Kristie

Kristin

Kristina

Krystal

Kyle

Kylie

Kyra

Lacey

Laddie

Laiken

Lala

Lana

Lance

Landon

Lane

Laney

Lantry

Laraine

Laramie

Laramy

Larissa

Larkin

Larry

Laura

Lauralee

Laureen

Laurel

Lauren

Lavelle

Lavender

Lavern

Law

Lawson

Layla

Leah

Leander

Lee

Leeanne

Lela

Leland

Lena

Lennie

Lenora

Leo

Leola

Leroy

Lesley

Leslie

Lester

Lettie

Levi

Lewis
Liam
Libby
Liberty
Lilac
Lili
Lillian
Lillie
Lilly
Lily
Lincoln
Linda
Lindsey
Lindsy
Lisa
Lisabeth
Lloyd
Logan
Lola
Londen
London
Loraine
Loralee
Loreen
Lorraine
Lory
Lottie
Lou
Louanne
Louie
Louis

Louisa
Lourdes
Lovett
Lowell
Lucas
Lucie
Lucille
Lucinda
Lucky
Lucretia
Lucy
Luella
Luke
Lula
Lulu
Lura
Luther
Lyda
Lydia
Lyle
Lyndall
Lyndon
Lynette
Lynn
Lynsey
Mabel
Mace
Macey
Mack
Mackenzie
Macy

Madaline

Madalyn

Maddie

Maddox

Madeline

Madelyn

Madison

Mae

Magenta

Maggie

Magnolia

Maisie

Major

Makayla

Malcolm

Malia

Malissa

Mallie

Mallory

Mame

Mammie

Mandy

Manuel

Maple

Maranda

Marcus

Marcy

Margaret

Marge

Margie

Margo

Margorie

Maria

Mariah

Mariam

Marianna

Maribel

Maribeth

Marie

Marigold

Marilyn

Marisol

Marissa

Mark

Marlene

Marley

Marlin

Marry

Marsh

Marsha

Marshall

Marta

Martha

Marti

Martin

Marty

Marvin

Mason

Mathew

Matilda

Matthew

Mattie

<table>
<tr><td>Maud</td><td>Michah</td></tr>
<tr><td>Maude</td><td>Micheal</td></tr>
<tr><td>Maureen</td><td>Michelle</td></tr>
<tr><td>Maurice</td><td>Mick</td></tr>
<tr><td>Maverick</td><td>Mickey</td></tr>
<tr><td>Mavis</td><td>Mickie</td></tr>
<tr><td>Max</td><td>Mika</td></tr>
<tr><td>Maxie</td><td>Mike</td></tr>
<tr><td>Maxine</td><td>Mila</td></tr>
<tr><td>Maxwell</td><td>Mildred</td></tr>
<tr><td>May</td><td>Miles</td></tr>
<tr><td>Maya</td><td>Miley</td></tr>
<tr><td>Maybelle</td><td>Milissa</td></tr>
<tr><td>Mazie</td><td>Milla</td></tr>
<tr><td>Mckenzie</td><td>Miller</td></tr>
<tr><td>Meagan</td><td>Millicent</td></tr>
<tr><td>Megan</td><td>Millie</td></tr>
<tr><td>Mel</td><td>Milly</td></tr>
<tr><td>Melissa</td><td>Milo</td></tr>
<tr><td>Melody</td><td>Mina</td></tr>
<tr><td>Melvin</td><td>Mindy</td></tr>
<tr><td>Mendy</td><td>Minerva</td></tr>
<tr><td>Meredith</td><td>Minnie</td></tr>
<tr><td>Merle</td><td>Miranda</td></tr>
<tr><td>Merlin</td><td>Miriam</td></tr>
<tr><td>Merrill</td><td>Mitch</td></tr>
<tr><td>Merry</td><td>Mitchell</td></tr>
<tr><td>Mia</td><td>Molly</td></tr>
<tr><td>Miah</td><td>Monica</td></tr>
<tr><td>Micah</td><td>Montana</td></tr>
<tr><td>Michael</td><td>Monte</td></tr>
</table>

Montgomery
Monty
Morgan
Morris
Muriel
Murphy
Myra
Myrtle
Nadine
Nancy
Naomi
Nash
Nat
Natalia
Natalie
Natasha
Nate
Nathan
Nathaniel
Nell
Nellie
Nelly
Nelson
Nettie
Neva
Newton
Nia
Nicholas
Nicky
Nicole
Nicolette

Nikki
Nina
Noah
Noel
Noelle
Nola
Nolan
Nora
Nova
Nyla
Obediah
Octavia
Odell
Odessa
Olga
Olive
Oliver
Olivia
Ollie
Opal
Ophelia
Ora
Orlando
Oroya
Orson
Oscar
Ossie
Owen
Ozzie
Paige
Paisley

Palmer
Pamela
Pansy
Paris
Parker
Particia
Pat
Patricia
Patrick
Pattie
Patty
Paul
Paula
Paulene
Paulette
Pauline
Paxton
Payton
Pearl
Peg
Peggie
Peggy
Penelope
Penny
Perry
Pete
Peter
Petrea
Peyton
Phebe
Philip

Phillis
Phobe
Phoebe
Phoenix
Pierce
Pike
Pink
Pinkie
Piper
Pippin
Polly
Porter
Powell
Presley
Preston
Pricilla
Priscilla
Prudence
Quentin
Quint
Rachael
Rachel
Raegan
Randall
Randy
Ranger
Raphael
Raven
Ray
Raymond
Reagan

Reba	Rosemary
Rebecca	Rosetta
Rebecka	Rosie
Red	Ross
Reed	Rowdy
Reese	Rowena
Remington	Roxanne
Rene	Roxie
Renee	Roxy
Reno	Roy
Rex	Royce
Rhett	Rozanne
Richard	Ruben
Ricky	Ruby
Ridley	Rudy
Riley	Ruger
Ringo	Russell
Rita	Russet
Robbie	Rusty
Robbin	Ruth
Robert	Ruthie
Robin	Ryan
Rochelle	Ryder
Rodeo	Rylie
Roderick	Sabastian
Roger	Sabrina
Ronnie	Sadie
Roper	Saffron
Rory	Sage
Rosa	Saige
Rose	Salina

Sallie
Sally
Sam
Samantha
Sammie
Sammy
Samuel
Sandy
Santiago
Sara
Sarah
Saunders
Savanna
Savannah
Sawyer
Scarlett
Scott
Scottie
Sean
Selina
Selma
Serenity
Seth
Shan
Shandi
Shane
Shannon
Shelby
Sherry
Shiloh
Shirley

Sidney
Sienna
Sierra
Silas
Silvana
Silvia
Simon
Simone
Sky
Skye
Skyler
Sofia
Sol
Sonny
Sonya
Sophia
Sophie
Stacey
Stacie
Stacy
Star
Stella
Stephen
Stephenie
Sterling
Stetson
Steven
Stevie
Storm
Suanne
Sue

Summer
Sunny
Susan
Susannah
Susanne
Sweeney
Sydney
Sylvie
Taggard
Taj
Tammy
Tanner
Tara
Tate
Tayler
Taylor
Teal
Teena
Teresa
Terrell
Terri
Terry
Tessa
Tessie
Tex
Thaddeus
Thaine
Thayne
Theo
Theodore
Theresa

Thomas
Thora
Thornton
Thurman
Tia
Tiffany
Tilda
Tillie
Tillman
Tilly
Tim
Timber
Timothy
Tina
Tinker
Tiny
Titus
Tobias
Toby
Tommy
Tony
Tonya
Tori
Tory
Trace
Tracy
Trapper
Travis
Trent
Trenton
Trevor

Trey	Victor
Tripp	Victoria
Tristan	Vikki
Troy	Vincent
Trudy	Vinnie
Truett	Viola
Truman	Violet
Tucker	Violette
Ty	Virgil
Tyce	Virginia
Tyler	Vivian
Tyson	Vonda
Ulysses	Vonnie
Ursula	Wade
Vada	Walker
Val	Wallace
Valarie	Wally
Vale	Walter
Vallie	Wanda
Vance	Ward
Vanessa	Warren
Vaughn	Waylon
Velma	Wayne
Vennie	Webb
Vera	Weldon
Vern	Wendell
Vernon	Wendy
Veronica	Wesley
Vesta	West
Vickie	Western Names
Vicky	Weston

Wheeler
Whitey
Whitley
Wilbur
Wilder
Wiley
Will
Willa
Willard
William
Williard
Willie
Willow
Wilma
Windy
Winnie
Winnifred
Winona
Winslow
Winston
Winter
Wister
Woody
Wyatt
Wylie
Xavier
Yasmin
Yasmine
Yvette
Yvone
Zachariah

Zachary
Zak
Zane
Zara
Zeb
Zed
Zeke
Zella
Zelma
Zinnia
Zoe
Zoey
Zora
Zylphia

URBAN & NICK NAMES

40 Khan
A'Mirayha
Aalissah
Aaliyah
Aaron
Aatisha
Ab
Ab-Soul
Abby
Abduiniana
Abdul
Abdullah
Abraham
Abrianna
Ace
Adaija
Adam
Adamari

Adarius
Addie
Aderian
Adina
Adonis
Adria
Adrian
Adriana
Adrianna
Adrien
Ahmad
Ahmead
Ahmed
Aiden
Aijon
Ailyn
Aisha
Aiyana

Aja
Ajalae
Ajay
Akeem
Akwon
Al
Al Bilal
Alan
Alana
Alasia
Alayah
Alaysia
Alazae
Aldrisha
Aleah
Alease
Alec
Alecia
Aleena
Aleisha
Alen
Aleshia
Alessandra
Alex
Alexa
Alexander
Alexia
Alexis
Alexus
Alexzander
Alfie

Alfonse
Alfonso
Alfonzo
Ali
Alia
Alicia
Alijah
Alique
Alisa
Alise
Alisha
Alison
Alissa
Alivia
Aliya
Aliyah
Alize'
Allan
Allegra
Allen
Allie
Ally
Allyn
Alnisa
Alona
Alonso
Alonzo
Alphonso
Althea
Altonisha
Alvaneisha

Alvin
Alvina
Alyce
Alycia
Alysa
Alyse
Alysha
Alysia
Alyson
Amanda
Amani
Amareon
Amari
Amarion
Amaury
Amaya
Amber
Ambiance
Ambrosia
Ameerah
Amel
Amelia
Amerie
Amethyst
Amil
Amillion
Amina
Amir
Amira
Amiri
Amiyah

Amonisha
Amor
Anae'sia
Anaejah
Andarius
Andre
Andrea
Andrecia
Andrew
Andria
André
Anette
Angel
Angela
Angelena
Angelica
Angelina
Angelique
Angie
Anisa
Anisha
Anissa
Anita
Aniya
Aniyah
Anjali
Ann
Anna
Annalisa
Annalise
Anne

Annette
Annie
Anquan
Ant
Ant Money
Antaneshia
Anthony
Antiniqua
Antione
Antionette
Antiqua
Antoine
Antoinette
Antonette
Antonio
Antonise
Antony
Antwan
Apache
Apollo
April
Apryl
Aquamarina
Arianna
Arianne
Arica
Arie
Arleen
Arlene
Armanda
Armani

Armelia
Arrin
Arron
Arshad
Artarius
Artavious
Artrell
Aryana
Aryanna
Asad
Ash
Asha
Ashad
Ashai
Ashanae
Ashante
Ashanti
Ashely
Ashirae
Ashlea
Ashlee
Ashleigh
Ashley
Ashli
Ashly
Ashton
Asia
Asia'nae
Asianna
Askari
Asley

Athea
Atiana
Attiyah
Attrell
Audante
Audel
Audrey
Aunt Berdie
Aura
Aushanique
Austin
Ava
Avantay
Aven
Avion
Avondre
Avonnah
Avonte
Ayana
Ayanna
Ayden
Aydin
Ayesha
Aylin
Azalee
Azmera
Azure
Azzie
B Black
B Chilli
B-Eazy

B.G.
Baby
Badda$$
Baeshawn
Bakari
Balinda
Ballah
Bam
Bammer
Bangga
Banks
Barbara
Barbeesha
Barbie
Barnard
Barnes
Barrie
Barron
Barry
Bas
Baseem
Bash
BashKisha
Bashonda
Bashquan
Basilia
Basim
Basimah
Beast
Beatrice
Bebe

Becki
Beckie
Becky
Bee
beezy
Bejani
Belamie
Belinda
Bella
Bellamey
Ben
Benita
Benjamin
Bennie
Benny
Bentley
Benz
Benzino
Beonnica
Berdella
Bernadette
Bernadine
Bernardina
Berneice
Bernetta
Bernice
Bernie
Berniece
Bernisha
Beronte
Berry

Berta
Bertha
Bertice
Bertie
Bess
Bessie
Bethea
Betricia
Betsey
Betsy
Bettie
Betty
Beverlee
Beverley
Beverly
Beyontsa
Bianca
Biara
Big Al
Big Boi
Big E
Big L
Big Mane
Big Que
Biggie
Bigz
Billz
Bira
Bird
Birdie
Bizarre

Bizz
Bizzy
BJ
Black
Blackman
Blade
Blanco
Blaq
Blaze
Blessing
Bloomp
Blu
Blue
Bo
Bobbie
Bocky
Bomani
Bon'Qui
Bon'Quisha
Bone
Boney
Bonifa
Bonita
Bonney
Bonnie
Bonny
Bonquisha
Boo
Boo Boo
Booba
Booby

Booker
Boom
Boon
Boop
Boosie
Boss
Boston
Boyah
Brandee
Brandi
Brandie
Brandon
Brandy
Brandyce
Braneisha
Braynell
Breana
Breann
Breanna
Breanne
Breasia
Breauntae
Bree
Breedz
Breesha
Breeze
Brejanay
Brenae
Brenda
Breshawna
Breyah

Breyelle
Bri-Bri
Bria
Brian
Brianda
Brianna
Brianne
Bridget
Bridgett
Bridgette
Brigette
Brinda
Brisk
Britany
Britney
Britni
Brittaney
Brittani
Brittanie
Brittany
Britteny
Brittney
Brittni
Brittny
Bronze
Brooklyn
Brooklynn
Bruse
Bryan
Bryanna
Bryant

Bryshaun
Buck
Bunny
Bunz
Bunz B
Burgundi
Busta
Butch
Byron
C Rac
C-God
C-Note
Cace
Caesar
Caeser
Cage
Cahil
Cahir
Cain
Caine
Cal
Calayah
Caleb
Cali
Callie
Calvin
Cam
Camaeron
Camara
Camden
Cameesha

Camelia
Camellia
Cameron
Camilla
Camille
Camillo
Camp
Camron
Candace
Candi
Candie
Candis
Candy
Canibus
Cannon
Capone
Capri
Caprice
Cara
Caren
Carey
Cari
Caricia
Carie
Carin
Carina
Carisa
Carissa
Carita
Carl
Carla

Carleen
Carlena
Carletta
Carlita
Carma
Carman
Carmel
Carmela
Carmelia
Carmella
Carmelo
Carmen
Carmina
Carmon
Carnell
Carol
Carolin
Carolina
Caroline
Caroll
Carolyn
Carolynn
Carreona
Carrol
Carroll
Carry
Carson
Cartrell
Caryn
Casandra
Case

Casey
Cash
Cashaun
Casie
Casimira
Cass
Cassandra
Cassey
Cassi
Cassidy
Cassie
Cassius
Cassondra
Cassy
Castor
Cat
Caterra
Catharine
Catherine
Catheryn
Cathey
Cathryn
Catina
Catrice
Catrina
Caydyn
Cayla
Cayvon
Cease
Cece
Cecilia

Cedric
Cedrick
Cee Lo
Cee-Lo
Celena
Celesta
Celeste
Celestina
Cesar
Chad
Chae
Chaleece
Chamique
Chance
Chandelle
Chandra
Chanel
Chanell
Chanelle
Chantay
Chante
Chantel
Chantell
Chantelle
Chaquell
Chardonnay
Charise
Charisma
Charissa
Charisse
Charita

Charity
Charleen
Charlena
Charlene
Charles
Charley
Charli
Charlie
Charlotte
Charmain
Charmaine
Charnae
Charritta
Chase
Chasidy
Chasity
Chassidy
Chastity
Chauncey
Chavontae
Chaya
Chayla
Chaz
Cheba
Chelsea
Chelsey
Chelsie
Chenari
Cher
Cherelle
Cherica

Cherilyn
Cherish
Cherlyn
Cherri
Cherrie
Cherry
Cherryl
Cheryl
Cheryle
Cheryll
Chetty
Chevy
Cheyanne
Chi
Chi-Chi
Chiddy
Chief
Chill
Chilli Chill
China
Chino
Chio
Chip
Chiquita
Chocolate
Choppa
Chris
Chrissy
Christal
Christeen
Christen

Christena
Christi
Christian
Christina
Christine
Christoper
Christopher
Chrystal
Chubbz
Chuck
Ciara
Ciera
Cierra
Cinnamon
Cinthia
Clarence
Claretha
Claretta
Clarice
Clarinda
Clarisa
Clarissa
Classie
Claude
Claudette
Claudia
Claudine
Cleo
Cleopatra
Clever
Clevon

Clipz
Clyde
Co Co
Coco
Coffee
Colby
Cole
Coletta
Colleen
Coltrane
Connie
Constance
Contessa
Cookie
Cooper
Cora
Coralee
Coralie
Corbin
Cordelia
Cordell
Coreen
Coretta
Corey
Cori
Corie
Corina
Corine
Corlissa
Cornelia
Cornelius

Cornell	Cyndy
Correion	Cynthia
Corrie	Cyrstal
Corrina	Cythia
Corrupt	D Ducketz
Cortney	D Lo
Cory	D'Andre
Countess	D'artagnan
Courtney	D'Launa
Craig	D'Shawn
Craze	D-Nice
Cris	Da'Niyah
Criss	Da'Quona
Cristal	Dacari
Cristen	Dachelle
Cristian	Daddy Man
Cristina	Daddy-O
Cristine	Daejanique
Cristopher	Daejuana
Crunk	Daesha
Crusher	Dafina
Cruz	Dahlia
Cruze	Daidryna
Crystal	Daimen
Crystle	Daine
Cuc	Daisha
Cuddy	Daitaivian
Curry	Daitrion
Curtis	Dakarai
Curtiss	Dakari
Cutty	Dalaya

Dale
Dallana
Dallas
Dalores
Damani
Damarcus
Damarion
Damaya
Damian
Damien
Damion
Damon
Damontae
Dana
Dane
Danelle
Danial
Daniel
Daniela
Daniele
Daniell
Daniella
Danielle
Danita
Danna
Dannette
Dannie
Dannielle
Danny
Danny Boi
Dante

Danyay
Danyel
Danyell
Danyelle
Daphine
Daphne
Daphnia
Daquan
Darcel
Darcell
Darcey
Darchelle
Darcie
Darcy
Dareisha
Darell
Daren
Darian
Dariana
Darien
Darin
Darius
Darleen
Darlene
Darlynn
Darmisha
Darnel
Darnell
Darnesha
Daron
Darran

Darrel
Darrell
Darren
Darreonna
Darrick
Darrin
Darrius
Darron
Darryl
Darryn
Darshae
Darshon
Darvell
Daryl
Darzaria
Dash
Dashawn
Dasia
Dasialena
Dauntrel
Dave
Davian
David
Davin
Davina
Davion
Davon
Davondre
Dawn
Dayana
Dayanara
Daylon
Dayna
Dayshanae
Dazzie
Dazzlyn
De'Lanice
Deacon
Deana
Deandra
DeAndre
Deandre
Deandrea
Deane
Deanne
Deanthony
Deb
Debbi
Debbie
Debbra
Debby
Debora
Deborah
Debra
Deck
Dee
Dee Dee
Deeann
Deeanna
Deedee
Deedra
Deena

Deezy
Def Thug
Deidra
Deion
Deja
DeKira
Del
Delaney
Delena
Delfina
Delia
Delisa
Dell
Delmar
Deloise
Delon
Delora
Deloras
Delorean
Delores
Deloris
Delphia
Delphine
Delveon
Delvin
Delvon
Delvonte
Demarcus
Demarion
Demarius
Demetrien

Demetrius
Demond
Dena
Deneen
Denice
Deniro
Denis
Denise
Denisha
Denita
Denna
Dennis
Denzel
Deon
Deonna
Deontae
Deonte
Dep
Derek
Derick
Derik
Derrick
Deryl
Desean
Deshaun
Deshawn
DeShawn
DeShay
Desirae
Desire
Desiree

Desmarae
Desmond
Destinee
Destiney
Destini
Destiny
Deuce
Dev
Devan
Devana
Deven
Deveon
Devin
Devlin
Devon
Devona
Devonte
Devyn
Dewayne
Deyanni
Diadora
Diamond
Diana
Diane
Dianna
Dianne
Diedra
Diedre
Dierdre
Diggs
Diggy

Diggy Choonz
Dilla
Dimitri
Dimples
Dina
Dinari
Dion
Dione
Dionna
Dionne
Diontray
Dirty
DiShae
Divina
Divine
Dizzee
Dizzy
Dmitri
Docta
Dog
Dolla
Dolores
Doloris
Dom
Domenic
Dominic
Dominik
Dominique
Domonique
Don Doddy
Dona

Donald
Donell
Donetta
Donette
Donna
Donnell
Donnetta
Donnette
Donnie
Donny
Dontasia
Dontavian
DonTayvia
Donte
Doobz
Doom
Doreen
Dorian
Dorris
Dorthy
Doug
Douglas
Douglass
Drama
Drave
Draven
Dre
Dreadz
Dro
Droop
Drop

Drusilla
Duane
Duante
Dubb
Dubz
Duck
Duffy
Duke
Dupri
Durantay
Durk
Dushawn
Duwaun
Duwayne
Dwaine
Dwayne
Dwhite
Dwight
Dylan
Dyllan
Dyllon
Dylon
Dymonique
Dynasty
Dyphia
D– Sheep
D'Keyah
E- Easy
Earl
Earlean
Earleen

Earlene
Easy Bee
Eazy
Ebbonasia
Ebonee
Eboni
Ebonie
Ebony
Echell
Echo
Eddie
Eddy
Edith
Edmari
Edmond
Edna
Edwin
Egypt
Eilene
El Boogie
Elaine
Elan
Eleanor
Eleanore
Elenora
Eli
Elijah
Eliot
Elisa
Elisabeth
Elisha
Elissa
Eliza
Elizabeth
Ella
Elle
Ellen
Elli
Elliot
Elliott
Ellis
Elois
Eloise
Elonda
Elroy
Elvin
Ely
Elyse
Emani
Emanuel
Emeka
Emerald
Emil
Emily
Emma
Emmanuel
Emogene
Empress
Enzo
Eric
Erica
Erick

Ericka
Erik
Erin
Erlene
Eros
Ervin
Erykah
Eshawn
Essence
Essie
Estell
Ester
Eternity
Ethan
Ethell
Eugene
Eula
Eureka
Eva
Evalyn
Evan
Eve
Evelyn
Everson
Evette
Evianna
Evon
Evonne
Exadria
Ezell
Fab

Factz
Fae
Faheem
Faith
Faiz
Famid
Fanita
Fannie
Fanny
Fantasia
Farah
Faris
Farrah
Farris
Farrontay
Fashawn
Fat Boy
Fat Dee
Fat Fat
Fatal K
Fatima
Fatimah
Fatisha
Fatz
Fawneice
Fay
Faye
Fe
Felecia
Felicia
Felisha

Felix
Felony
Fetty
Fiasco
Finesse
Five
Flame
Flav
Flex
Flora
Florance
Florence
Floresha
Floss Boy
Fly Cat
Fo'Landra
Foxx
Foxxy
Foxy
Frajon
Fran
France
Francella
Francene
Frances
Francis
Frank
Freak
Freaky
Fred
Freddie

Freddy
Frederic
Frederica
Frederick
Fredonia
Fredresia
Fredric
Fredrika
Free
Freesia
French Boy
Freonte
Fresh
Frost
Funny
Future
Fuze
Fuzz
G
Gab
Gabby
Gabriael
Gabriel
Gabrielle
Gage
Gail
Gale
Galena
Gardell
Garnett
Garrett

Garry	Gianni
Gary	Gibbs
Gater	Giggs
Gayle	Gilbreona
Gearldine	Gina
Gee-Gee	Ginger
Gemini	Gino
Gemma	Giovani
Gene	Giovanna
Genesis	Giovanni
Geneva	Giovoni
Genie	Gipp
Genique	Gipsy
Genoveva	Giselle
George	Gladis
Georgeann	Gladys
Georgeanna	Glenda
Georgia	Glinda
Georgiana	Glock
Georgianna	Gloria
Gerald	Glory
Geraldine	Goldie
Germain	Grace
Germaine	Graham
Gerri	Graig
Gerry	Gram
Gertude	Grand B
Gervonte	Grandz
Gia	Grayce
Gian	Greg
Gianna	Gregory

Grimm
Groove
Gunna
Gunz
Gunz P
Gwen
Haamid
Haddi
Haiz
Haize
Hakeem
Hakeisha
Hakim
Hallie
Halo
Hamad
Hamal
Hamid
Hamisha
Hammer
Harmony
Harper
Harrell
Harriet
Harriett
Harriette
Hasana
Hasani
Hassan
Hattie
Haven

Havoc
Hawk
Hayden
Haze
Hazel
Heaven
Heavenly
Heemy
Helen
Helena
Hellen
Hemisha
Hennessy
Henney
Herb
Honey
Hook
Hope
Hoya
Hurricane
Hush
Hydia
Hykeem
Hype
I'Shauna
Ibn
Ice
Idell
Idrease
Idreece
Idrees

Idriece
Iesha
Iggy
Ijanea
Ike
Ikeyla
Ilene
Illy Boi
Ilonna
Imani
Imanual
Imanuel
Immanuel
Imogene
Imondre
Inayah
India
Indigo
Indira
Inez
Infamous
Infamous Face
Ionna
Irene
Iris
Irish
Irvine
Isaac
Isabell
Isabella
Isabelle

Isadora
Isaiah
Ishaan
Ishmael
Ishmel
Isiah
Isis
Ismael
Israel
Issac
Ivan
Ivanna
Iverson
Iveryana
Ivey
Ivonne
Ivory
Ivy
Iyanna
Iyanya
Izabella
Izaiah
J'varean
J-Five
J-Vibe
Ja Breezy
Ja'Darius
Ja'Maia
Jaasen
Jaavon
Jab

Jabari	Jae-Naj
Jabarri	Jaeden
Jabeerah	Jaelynn
Jabir	Jafaysha
Jabiri	Jahari
Jabree	Jaheed
Jabrielle	Jaheem
Jacalyn	Jaheim
Jace	Jahfee
Jacelyn	Jahlil
Jacin	Jahtay
Jacinda	Jahzara
Jackelyn	Jai
Jackie	Jaida
Jackquelin	Jaiden
Jacob	Jaime
Jacqualin	Jaimee
Jacquan	Jaimie
Jacquees	Jaiviana
Jacquel	Jakai
Jacquelin	Jakayla
Jacqueline	Jakaylon
Jacquise	Jakori
Jada	Jalayah
Jadan	Jaleesa
Jadarius	Jalen
Jade	Jalisa
Jaden	Jaliyah
Jadin	Jalyn
Jadyn	Jalynn
Jae	Jamaal

Jamal
Jamar
Jamarcus
Jamaree
Jamari
Jamarion
Jameeka
Jamel
James
Jamey
Jami
Jamie
Jamier
Jamil
Jamila
Jamill
Jamiqua
Jamir
Jamise
Jamison
Jamya
Janae
Janasha
Janay
Jane
Janean
Janeen
Janel
Janell
Janelle
Janessa

Janet
Janett
Janetta
Janiah
Janice
Janiel
Janis
Janiya
Janiyah
Jannet
Jannette
Janyce
JaNyla
Japri
Jaquan
Jaquana
Jaquanda
Jaquandria
Jaqueline
Jaquelyn
Jaquetta
Jaquez
Jaquin
Jared
Jareem
Jarell
Jaren
Jarius
Jarod
Jaron
Jaronda

Jarred	Jaye
Jarren	Jayla
Jarrett	Jaylan
Jarrod	Jaylen
Jascenda	Jaylin
Jase	Jaylisa
Jasmin	Jaylon
Jasmine	Jaylyn
Jasmyn	Jaylynn
Jason	Jayo
Jatavauis	Jayrel
Jaunita	Jayson
Javae	Jayvion
Javan	Jayzel
Javaris	Jazanae
Javarr	Jazlyn
Javen	Jazmin
Javia	Jazmine
Javier	Jazmyn
Javion	Jazz
Javon	Jazz-E
Javonda	Jazzie
Javonna	Jazznifa
Javonte	Ja'Quandria
Jay	Jeane
Jay Rock	Jeanelle
Jayce	Jeanette
Jayda	JeBron
Jayden	Jeff
Jaydin	Jefferey
Jaydon	Jeffery

Jeffrey
Jem
Jenelle
Jeneva
Jeraldine
Jeramy
Jeremiah
Jeremy
Jeri
Jerieasha
Jermaine
Jermika
Jerome
Jeronda
Jerrell
Jerrice
Jerrod
Jerry
Jesse
Jessica
Jessika
Jevan
Jevontae
Jevontaye
Jevonte
Jewel
Jewell
Jha'Bria
Jharell
Jhevanise
Jhimain

Jhirmaine
Jikai
Jikal
Jimar
Jimmie
Jimmy
Jin
Jiri
Jivonte
Jo
Jo Jo
Joakim
Joan
Joanna
Joanne
Joaquin
Joc
Jocelyn
Jock
Jocob
Jodee
Jodey
Jodi
Jodie
Jody
Joe
Joedi
Joedy
Joel
Joell
Joelle

Joenae
Joesph
Joey
Johanna
John
Johnathan
Johnathon
Johnavon
Johnna
Johnnie
Johnny
Johntae
Joi
Jolie
Jon
Jonathan
Jonathon
Jonelle
JonTonae
Jordan
Jordyn
Jorge
Josef
Josefine
Joseph
Josephine
Josh
Joshua
Josiah
Jospeh
Jovan

Jovani
Jovanni
Jovanny
Jovany
Joy
Joyce
Joycelyn
Jo'Minique
Ju Ju
Juan
Juanita
Juicy
Jules
Julian
Julien
Juliet
Julio
Julious
Julius
June
June Bug
June-bug
Junior
Justice
Justin
Justus
Juwitta
Jy'Den
Jyneshia
Ka'Lifah
Kabir

Kace
Kacee
Kade
Kadeem
Kadeer
Kaden
Kadin
Kadir
Kaeden
Kaelyn
Kahill
Kahnie
Kai
Kaid
Kaiden
Kaijuan
Kailil
Kailin
Kain
Kaine
Kaj
Kalan
Kalandria
Kalani
Kalayah
Kaleel
Kaliko
Kalil
Kalisha
Kaliyah
Kalon

Kalvin
Kam
Kamari
Kamarion
Kameisha
Kameron
Kamilah
Kamilla
Kamiya
Kamron
Kamryn
Kamyria
Kandace
Kandi
Kandis
Kandy
Kane
Kane[1]
Kaneesha
Kanesha
Kanika
Kanisha
Kannon
Kanye
Kara
Kareem
Kareen
Karen
Karima
Karina
Karissa

Karzell
Kasandra
Kaseem
Kasey
Kash
Kashawna
Kashayla
Kasheem
Kashif
Kason
Kass
Kassidy
Kastro
Kat
Katarina
Katavia
Kataya
Kathleen
Katima
Katina
Katreen
Katrina
Kaveon
Kavonte
Kay
Kay Kay
Kayauna
Kayden
Kaydra
Kaye
Kayla

Kaylah
Kaylee
Kayson
Kayundra
Ke'Von
Kea
KeAir
Keaton
Keef
Keenan
Keenon
Keesha
Keife
Keira
Keisha
Keith
Kelaiah
Kelendria
Kelis
Kelley
Kelly
Kellz
Kelsey
Kelvianna
Kelvin
Kemberly
Kemontay
Ken
Ken'Trice
Kenan
Kendal

Kendall	Kha'Jae
Kendra	Khadijah
Kendria	Khalid
Kendrick	Khalil
Kenesha	Khalilah
Keneth	Khan
Keni	Khia
Kenisha	Ki Ki
Kenitra	Kia
Kenneth	Kian
Kennith	Kiana
Kenny	Kianna
Kentrell	Kiara
Kenya	Kidd
Kenyatta	Kiera
Kenyetta	Kieran
Kenyon	Kierra
Keon	Kiesha
Kerry	Kieth
Keshawn	Kiki
Ketara	Killa
Keven	Killa Mike
Kevin	Killa Rah
Kevon	Killah
Kevonte	Kilo
Keylaysha	Kim
Keyon	Kimaria
Keysha	Kimberlaine
Keyshawn	Kimberley
Keyshia	Kimberly
Keyz	Kimi

Kimmy
Kimone
Kimora
Kina
Kindra
King
King Mac
King-Matic
Kingston
Kiniyah
Kira
Kiran
Kisha
Kitty
Knocc Out
Koffee
Kokane
Kool Dude
Korey
Kori
Kortney
Kory
Kourtney
Kraig
Kramisha
Krayzie
Kris
Krishaun
Kristal
Kristan
Kristen

Kristian
Kristofer
Kristopher
Krush
Kudrow
Kuntry
Kurtis
Kuttz
Kwame
Kwan
Kwanisha
Kween
Kweli
Kwon
Ky-Azia
Kya
Kyan
Kylan
Kyle
Kyliana
Kymberly
Kyra
Kyree
Kyren
Kyrin
K'wan
L Roc
La La
La'Kisha
La'Kya
La'Quaysha

La'Quishria
La'shanae
La'Taniana
La'Tanya
La'Trice
Labeef
LaBreya
Labron
Lacy
Ladarius
Ladasha
Ladaysha
Laila
Laisha
Lajontay
Lakayla
Lakeesha
Lakeisha
Lakendra
Lakenya
Lakesha
Lakeshia
Lakia
Lakiesha
Lakisha
Lakshya
Lala
Lamar
Lamarr
Lamia
Lamirisha

Lamiyah
Lamonica
Lamont
Lamonte
Lance
Laneice
Lanelle
Laneshia
Lanessa
Lanette
Lanora
Laquan
Laquanda
LaQueisha
Laquisha
Laquita
Lara
Laraine
Larion
Larisa
Larissa
Laronda
Larraine
Larry
Lasandra
Lashala
Lashanda
Lashandra
Lashaun
Lashawn
Lashawna

LaShawnda	Lauryn
Lashay	Lavelle
Lashell	Lavenia
Lashon	Lavern
Lashonda	Laverne
Latanya	Lavette
Latarsha	Lavina
Latasha	Lavinia
Latesha	Lavon
Latia	Lavonda
Laticia	Lavone
Latifa	Lavonna
Latifah	Lavonne
Latisha	Lawana
Latonia	Lawanda
Latonya	Lawanna
Latosha	Lawerence
Latoya	Lawrence
Latoyia	Layla
Latrell	Layontae
Latrevion	Le Le
Latrice	Lea
Latricia	Leah
Latrina	Lean
Latrisha	Leandrenae
Laura	Leanne
Lauralee	Leanora
Laurashay	Leatrice
Laureen	Ledontae
Lauren	Lee
Laurence	Leela

Leena
Legit
LeJon
Lekisha
Lelah
Lenique
Lennie
Lenny
Lenora
Lenore
Leo
Leon
Leonarda
Leonore
LeRon
Leroy
Les
Leshawna
Leshay
Lesley
Leslie
Letesha
Lethal
Letisha
Letitia
Lettie
Levar
Levell
Levester
Levi
LeVon

Levondia
Lewis
Lex
Lexi
Lexie
Lexus
Lezlie
Lianne
Lilah
Lillian
Lilliana
Lil' Deuce
Lil' Flip
Lil' Killah
Lil' Thug
Linda
Lindsey
Linette
Lino
Lionel
Liquisha
Lisa
Lisabeth
Lisandra
Lissa
Livia
Liz
Lizzette
Lizzie
Lizzy
Li' Diggs

Lloyd
Loco
Loddi
Lofanna
Logan
Logic
Lois
Loise
Lola
Lolita
Londa
London
Londrea
Loni
Lonnie
Lonny
Lontrel
Loon
Lora
Loraine
Loralee
Lord
Loren
Lorene
Loretta
Lori
Lorie
Lorraine
Lorretta
Lory
Lottie

Louanne
Louella
Louis
Love
Low-key
Loyd
Lucas
Lucile
Lucilla
Lucille
Lucinda
Lucrecia
Lucretia
Luella
Lump
Lurlene
Luther
Lydell
Lydia
Lyfe
Lyle
Lynda
Lynell
Lynette
Lynice
Lynn
Lynnda
Lynnette
Lyric
Lyrics
Ma'nisha

Mabel

Mabelle

Mable

Mac

Mac Gee

Maccey

Mace

Macey

Machelle

Macie

Mack

Mackey

Mackie

Mackinzie

Macy

Mad Boi

Maddie

Madea

Mae

Maegan

Maggi

Magic

Mahoganie

Mahogany

Maisha

Majenae

Major

Makaila

Makayla

Makenna

Malachi

Malaysia

Maleshia

Malice

Malik

Malinda

Malissa

Mally

Mammie

Man

Man-Man

Maniqua

Mannie

Manny

Manual

Manuel

Marc

Marcel

Marcell

Marcella

Marcellus

Marci

Marcia

Marcie

Marcus

Marcy

Maria

Mariah

Marie

Marilyn

Marina

Marinda

Mario
Marion
Marisa
Marissa
Marjani
Mark
Markaya
Markayla
Markell
Marketta
Markie
Markita
Markus
Marky
Marlee
Marleen
Marley
Marlin
Marlo
Marlon
Marquai
Marquaine
Marques
Marquette
Marquez
Marquis
Marquise
Marquita
Marsavius
Marshae
Martini

Martinique
Martrell
Marvin
Mary
Mary-Jane
Marz
Marí
Maserati
Mashonda
Mason
Mathew
Matt
Matthew
Mattie
Maureen
Maurice
Mavis
Maxie
Maxima
Maxine
May
Maya
Mazarae
Maze
Mckayla
Mckenna
Mckenzie
Meagan
Mecca
Mechelle
Meena

Megan	Michelle
Meia	Micky
Mel	Miesha
Melanie	Miguel
Melany	Mika
Melina	Mikaeja
Melinda	Mikaela
Melissa	Mikayla
Mello	Mike
Melodee	Mikel
Melodie	Mikey
Melody	Milan
Melonie	Miles
Melony	Miliani
Melvin	Milissa
Memphis	Milk
Mercedes	Mill
Merissa	Milla
Mesha	Milly
Meshell	Milo
Meyasha	Milton
Mi'Quel	Mimi
Mia	Minister
Micah	Minnie
Michael	Miracle
Michal	Miriam
Michale	Misha
Micheal	Missy
Michel	Mista
Michele	Mitch
Michell	Mitchel

Mitchell	Murder
Mitchy	My'Leah
Mo'Nique	Mya
Mock Moo	Myah
Moe	Myeasha
Mohamed	Myeisha
Mohammad	Myesha
Mohammead	Myiesha
Mohammed	Myka
Moka	Myles
Mona	Myonna
Monaray	Myriah
Moneesha	Myrna
Monet	Myron
Money	Myrtle
Monica	Mystique
Monifa	N9ne
Monika	Na'Kayla
Monique	Na'shantae Oasis
Monisha	Na'Zarah
Monnie	Na'Zyia
Montanae	Nadene
Montayah	Nadia
Montesha	Nadine
Montray	Nadirah
Monty	Naj
Mookie	Najahni
Morgan	Najim
Moriah	Nakeisha
Muhammad	Nakesha
Murda	Nakia

Nakisha

Nakita

Nancee

Nancey

Nancie

Nancy

Nannette

Naomi

Naquante

Narik

Narinna

Nas

Nash

Nashaun

Nashaya

Nashayda

Nasir

Nasty

Natacha

Natalee

Natalia

Natalie

Natalya

Natasha

Natashia

Nate

Nathan

Nathanael

Nathanial

Nathaniel

Natharious

Nathen

Natisha

Natissha

Natosha

Naveah   (Heaven spelled backwards)

Navon

Naykeisha

Nayquanna

Ne Ne

Neeshia

Neferteri

Neno

Neosha

Nessa

Netta

Nette

Nettie

Nevaeh   (heaven spelled backwards)

Nia

Nicandra

Nichelle

Nicholas

Nichole

Nick

Nicki

Nickie

Nickolas

Nickole

Nicky

Nicola
Nicolas
Nicole
Nicolette
Nicolle
Niesha
Nika
Niki
Nikia
Nikita
Nikki
Nikkimah
Nikole
Nila
Niles
Nimisha
Nina
Nipsey
Nisha
Nita
Niya
Noel
Noelle
Nola
Nora
Norma
Norvell
Nu-Nu
Nubian
Nugget
Nutty
Nya
Nyah
Nyasia
Nyce
Nyelle
Nyianna
Nykesha
Nyla
Nyranna
O
O B
Ocatavious
Oceana
Octavia
Octavier
Odell
Oderius
Odessa
Ofelia
Olivia
Omar
Omari
Omarion
Omeisha
Oneasha
Onika
Onyx
Ophelia
Orcasia
Orellius
Ornella

Orrese
Oshae
Oshea
Otis
Ottacious
Owen
Ox
Pace
Pam
Pamala
Pamela
Pamella
Pandora
Paris
Particia
Passion
Pat
Patience
Patrice
Patricia
Patrick
Patrina
Patrisha
Patrone
Patti
Paul
Paula
Paulene
Paulette
Peach
Peaches

Pearl
Pearline
Pebbles
Penney
Penny
Percy
Pernell
Perri
Perry
Pershon
Persia
Pete
Petrina
Pharoah
Phil
Philip
Phillip
Phillis
Phoenix
Phylicia
Phylis
Phyllis
Pierce
Pierre
Pierson
Pinky
Poet
Polo
Poob
Pooch
Pooh

Pookey
Pop
Porsche
Porsha
Porshia
Portia
Posh
Prada
Prayana
Preacher
Precious
Preme
Prentiss
Preston
Prez
Pricilla
Priest
Prince
Princess
Priscena
Priscila
Priscilla
Prodigy
Promise
Pryde
Purrp
Pusha
Qiana
Qiwan
Quaasia
Quabil

Quadeer
Quadim
Quadir
Quadre
Quadrees
Quadria
Quaisha
Qualyn
Quamar
Quan
Quanae
Quandell
Quandra
Quanell
Quanice
Quanisha
Quanna
Quannel
Quannell
Quantae
Quantay
Quantell
Quantez
Quarren
Quarron
Quasean
Quashaan
Quashan
Quashaun
Quashaw
Quashawn

Quashay
Quasheem
Quashon
Quasim
Quayana
Que'Shayda
Queen
Quenel
Quennel
Quentasia
Quenten
Quentin
Quenton
Quest
Queyona
Quiandra
Quik
Quil
Quill
Quin
Quin'Nya
Quince
Quincey
Quincy
Quindarius
Quinta
Quintavius
Quinten
Quintin
Quinton
Quintrell

Quizz
Quontavious
Quvontay
Qyree
Rab
Rachael
Rachel
Rachelle
Rackesha
Racquel
Rae Quan
Raekwon
Rafael
Rage
Rah
Raheem
Rahsaan
Rahul
Rainelle
Rainey
Rainy
Raj
Rajan
Rajeesh
Rakisha
Ralph
Ram
Rameel
Ramiro
Ramon
Ramona

<table>
<tr><td>

Rampage
Ramses
Ramsey
Ranasha
Randal
Randall
Randell
Randolph
Randy
Raniya
Raphael
Raquel
Rasha
Rashad
Rashan
Rashanda
Rashard
Rasheeda
Rashid
Rashida
Rashonda
Ratasha
Raul
Raven
Ravi
Ray
Ray Ray
Raye
Raymon
Raymond
Raynelle

</td><td>

Raynique
Rayshawn
Rayven
Raz
Reba
Rebecca
Rebecka
Rebekah
Rebel
Red
Redbone
Redd
Reece
Reed
Reek
Reese
Reggie
Regina
Reginald
Reid
Rell
Remmy
Remo
Rene
Renesia
Rene'
Renielle
Renita
Reno
Renzo
Rey

</td></tr>
</table>

Reyvion
Rhianna
Rhoda
Rhonda
Rhys
Rian
Rican
Rich
Rich Boi
Richard
Richelle
Richie
Rick
Rickey
Rickie
Ricky
Rider
Rihanna
Riley
Rio
Rita
Ritz
Rizzo
Rob
Robbie
Robby
Robert
Robin
Robyn
Rocco
Rochelle
Rock
Rocky
Rod
Roddy
Rodney
Rodrick
Roland
Rolanda
Rolla
Romanda
Rome
Romelle
Romeo
Romona
Ron
Ron Gotti
Ronald
Ronda
Rone
Roniesha
Ronnetta
Ronnie
Ronny
Roots
Rosalind
Rosalyn
Roscoe
Rose
Roselee
Roshandra
Roshaun

Rosslyn
Rowdy
Roxanne
Roxie
Roxy
Roy
Roya
Royal
Royce
Rozanda
Rozanne
Ruben
Rubie
Rubin
Ruby
Rude Boi
Ruff
Rugga
Ruquayah
Rush
Russel
Russell
Ruth
Ryah
Ryan
Rydah
Rylan
Sa'id
Saadiq
Sabrina
Sacha

Sade
Sadie
Sadistic
Saedi
Saffron
Safiya
Sahara
Sal
Saladine
Salina
Sam
Samantha
Samara
Samaria
Samid
Samir
Samira
Sammie
Sammy
Samson
Samual
Samuel
Sandra
Saniya
Saniyah
Sapphire
Saquisha
Sara
Sarafenia
Sarah
Saraya

Sariah
Sarina
Sasha
Savage
Savana
Savanah
Savanna
Savannah
Saviere
Savion
Scoobz
Scoota
Scooter
Scott
Scottie
Scotty
Scrap
Screwz
Sean
Sebrina
Sekeya
Selena
Semaj
Semora
Sequayah
Serenella
Serenity
Sha
Sha Money
Sha'Bria
Sha'Londria

Sha'Niquia
Sha'Quonda
Sha'Tanya
Sha'Zyah
Sha-Kiki
Shad
Shadae
Shade
Shadow
Shadray
Shadre
Shady
Shae
Shaheed
Shaina
Shakeerah
Shakeria
Shakia
Shakienah
Shakila
Shakira
Shakita
Shakiya
Shakur
Shala
Shalanda
Shalandra
ShaLaunda
Shalita
Shalonda
Shamal

Shamar
Shamaria
Shamecca
Shameek
Shameeka
Shameel
Shameka
Shamese
Shamika
Shammeka
Shamonica
Shan
Shanae
Shanda
Shandra
Shane
Shaneetta
Shaneice
Shanel
Shanell
Shani
Shania
Shanice
Shanika
Shaniqua
Shanique
Shanisha
Shanita
Shaniya
Shankeysha
Shannan

Shannon
Shanon
Shanquilla
Shantae
Shantay
Shante
Shantel
Shantell
Shantelle
Shantequa
Shantique
Shaquan
Shaquana
Shaquanisha
Shaquanna
Shaquasia
Shaquille
Shaquita
Shaquitta
Shaquonda
Shaquoya
Shar'Meisha
Sharday
Sharee
Shareef
Shareek
Shareem
Sharell
Sharen
Shari
Sharice

Sharie
Shariella
Sharika
Sharleen
Sharlene
Sharmaine
Sharmillah
Sharnae
Sharnell
Sharolyn
Sharon
Sharonda
Sharonica
Sharri
Sharron
Shartavia
Sharyl
Sharyn
Shasandra
Shatana
Shatika
Shatone
Shatwana
Shaun
Shauna
Shauneika
Shaunte
Shauntice
Shauntraneice
Shavadria
Shavon

Shavonda
Shavondrea
Shavonne
Shaw
Shawanda
Shawn
Shawna
Shawnda
Shawndra
Shawnee
Shawnie
Shawnna
Shawty
Shay
Shayla
Shayna
Shayne
Shea
Sheba
Sheek
Sheeka
Sheem
Sheena
Sheila
Sheilah
Shelby
Sheldon
Shelley
Shelly
Shelton
Shena

Shenetta
Sheree
Sherell
Sherice
Sherise
Sherita
Sherlene
Sherley
Sherly
Sherman
Shermanda
Shernell
Sheron
Sherrell
Sherry
Sheryl
Shiana
Shiela
Shine
Shira
Shirely
Shirleen
Shirley
Shock P
Shocka
Shokka
Shomari
Shon
Shonda
Shondreka
Shonique
Shontay
Shontaye
Shontel
Shorty
Shorty Roc
Shug
Shyann
Shyanne
Shyla
Shyne
Sibyl
Sid
Sidney
Sienna
Sierra
Silvana
Silver
Silvia
Simon
Simona
Simone
Sincere
Sir
Skeet
Sky
Skylar
Skyler
Slam
Slaughter
Slay Swagga
Sleepy

Slick
Slick Dizzle
Slick Dollah
Slim
Slow
Smitty
Smooth
Snake
Sneed
So-So
Sofia
Solo
Son
Sonali
Sondra
Sonja
Sonya
Sophia
Sophie
Soul
Soulja
Sparkle
Spyda
Stacey
Stacie
Stacy
Star
Starkeisha
Starkesha
Starlisha
Starr

Stax
Steel
Stefani
Stefanie
Stefany
Stefonte
Stella
Stephani
Stephanie
Stephen
Stephon
Steve
Steven
Stevie
Stone
Stones
Storm
Stretch
Strutz
Stunna
Styles
Sue-Ella
Suga
Sukari
Summer
Sunny
Supreme
Susan
Sushaunna
Swerve
Swift

Swizz
Swoop
Sydney
Sydnie
Syleena
Sylvia
Symone
Symphony
Synthia
T'Marius
T-Non
Ta'Nae
Tabi
Tabitha
Tah
Tahiem
Tahlay
Taisha
Tajanae
Takanisha
Takeisha
Takeshia
Takiella
Takisha
Talan
Talandria
Talin
Talisha
Talitha
Taliyah
Tallen

Talon
Tamala
Tamar
Tamara
Tamarah
Tameka
Tamesha
Tamia
Tamika
Tamilla
Tamiqua
Tamiya
Tammara
Tammie
Tammy
Tanasha
Tanasia
Taneadra
Tanequa
Tanesha
Tangela
Tanicia
Taniquia
Tanisha
Taniya
Taniyah
Tanja
Tanya
Tanyelle
Taquasia
Taquila

Taquilla

Taqweeshea

Tara

Tarah

Tarana

Taria

Tariq

Tarius

Tasha

Tashanni

Tasheema

Tasheona

Tashon

Tasia

Tatalisha

Tatanesha

Tataquisha

Tateeshia

Tatiana

Tationna

Tatiyanna

Tatyana

Tavion

Tawanda

Tay

Tay Tay

Taylona

Taylor

Tayontay

Tayquan

Tazaria

Ta'Jah

Teairra

Tedashii

Teddy

Tee

Teena

Teisha

Tek

Telesia

Temika

Tempa

Temple

Tenayla

Tenisha

Teontay

Tequila

Tera

Terence

Teresa

Teri

Terrance

Terrell

Terrence

Terri

Terria

Terrion

Terry

Tessa

Tevin

Teyana

Thadisha

Theandre
Theo
Theresa
Thomas
Thomasena
Thomasina
Thurman
Tia
Tianna
Tiara
Tiberius
Tical
Tierra
Tiesha
Tiffany
Tiheerah
Tillionna
Timarius
Timaya
Timothy
Tina
Tinie
Tinisha
Tiny
Tionne
Tiontae
Tish
Tisha
Tivon
Tniqua
Todd

Tommie
Tommy
Tone
Tonee
Tonesha
Toney
Toni
Tonia
Tonischa
Tonisha
Tontalisha
Tony
Tonya
Toquesha
Toquita
Torch
Torey
Tori
Torin
Toronda
Torrance
Torrey
Torry
Tory
Tosh
Tovel
Tra'Kiria
Tra'Naija
Tra'Vious
Trace
Tracey

Tracie

Tracy

Tradarious

Trae

Tramaine

Trameeca

Tramyara

Traniece

Trap

Trashaun

Travaun

Travion

Travis

Travon

Travus

Travuss

Tray

Traylora

Trayshia

Tre

Treasure

Trel

Tremain

Tremaine

Tremane

Tremayne

Trenay

Trevell

Trever

Trevion

Trevon

Trevor

Trey

Trey Shavondre

Treyanna

Treymeer

Trianna

Trickz

Trigg

Trigga

Trillz

Trina

Trinity

Tris

Trish

Trisha

Tristan

Tristen

Tristian

Tristin

Troi

Trouble

Troy

True

Trymeisha

Tryshelle

Trystan

Tuan

Tumika

Tunes

Twan

Twanesha

Tweet	Tyronda
Tweety	Tyrone
Twinky	Tyshawn
Twist	Tyshaye
Twists	Tyshiea
Ty	Tyson
Ty'Aira	T'kwon
Ty'Zaria	Udama
Tyanne	Udell
Tydarius	Ufonda
Tyesha	Ulainna
Tyisha	Ulises
Tylan	Umar
Tyler	Unae
Tylor	Uniqua
Tynessa	Unique
Tynique	Urban
Tynisha	Uzhanay
Tyquadia	V'Lanta
Tyquan	Val
TyQuan	Valarie
TyQuanda	Valencia
Tyquandria	Valeri
Tyra	Valerie
Tyree	Valia
Tyreeq	Vaneka
Tyreese	Vanessa
Tyrell	Vanetta
Tyrese	Vania
Tyrika	Vanisha
Tyron	Vanita

Vanity
Vanna
Vannessa
Vegas
Velonda
Velvet
Vence
Venessa
Venom
Venus
Verna
Verneisha
Vernell
Vernetta
Vernon
Veronica
Vershaun
Vic
Vice
Vick
Vickie
Vicky
Victor
Victoria
Vill
Vince
Vincent
Vivian
Vivica
Von
Von'dre

Vonetta
Vonreeta
Vontavia
Vonte
Vontray
Vontrice
Vonzella
Walandra
Wallace
Wallisha
Wally
Wanda
Wanetta
Wanishia
Wanita
Washondria
Wayne
Waynice
Wendella
Wendy
Wesley
West
Westion
Whitney
Wicks
Wil
Will
Willaysia
Willena
William
Willie

Willy
Wilma
Wilmarie
Wilshara
Windell
Winn
Winter
Wolf
Wonda
Wonk
Woo
Wykeisha
Wyneisha
Wynell
Wynisha
Wyontae
Xanaiya
Xaquita
Xaukeria
Xavier
Xavion
Xavius
Xolaya
Xzavier
Xzavinesha
Ya Ya
Yahir
Yakeisha
Yakim
Yakira
Yalasia
Yamal
Yamarra
Yanique
Yanni
Yaquan
Yara
Yasheef
Yashika
Yasin
Yasir
Yasmin
Yasmine
Yatima
Yavonte
Yazmin
Yervand
Yevette
Ymani
Yogi
Yolanda
Yolonda
Yonette
Yontay
Yorick
Yosef
Yosh
Yoshi
Yoshie
Young Boi
Young Kuts
Young Rell

Yovana
Yovany
YoYo
Yudell
Yuri
Yvette
Yvone
Yvonne
Zaccardi
Zachary
Zachery
Zahina
Zahmirie
Zahquasia
Zaiden
Zakiyyah
Zakwan
Zamaria
Zamine
Zamir
Zanaya
Zaniqua
Zaniya
Zaquan
Zaquisha
Zara
Zaria
Zariah
Zarion
Zarvontae
Zavier

ZaVon
Zay'Vionne
Zaybreon
Zayden
Zaylin
Zayshawn
Za'ire
Zeandre
Zeke
Zenarae
Zenobia
Zenzelle
Zeontae
Zeshawn
Zhane
Zhauntazia
Ziberia
Ziere
Ziggy
Zishan
Zock
Zoe
Zohneice
Zonnique
Zontae
Zontay
Zoo
Zora
Zuri
Zyaire
Zylen

Zynell
Zyreah

BOOKS BY ANGEL B

THE TASE MEN SERIES

Loving Rainy Days Vol. 1
Exerpt
Amazon: http://tinyurl.com/7k8cgxl

Michael's Heat Vol. 2
Excerpt
Amazon: http://tinyurl.com/michaelsheat

Up For The Chase Vol. 3
Excerpt
Amazon: http://tinyurl.com/ogm4klv

Child Support
Excerpt
Amazon: http://tinyurl.com/7pl839r

Unstable creature
Excerpt
Amazon: http://tinyurl.com/unstablecreature

The 7th Commandment (Novelette)
Amazon: http://tinyurl.com/la59s7g

SHORT STORIES
I Must Be Crazy Series

My Masked Lover Episode 1
Amazon: http://tinyurl.com/bymnyru

Teacher's Pet Episode 2
Amazon: http://tinyurl.com/ah7j93q

Daily Dose Episode 3
Amazon: http://tinyurl.com/n8oxbbd

SOCIAL MEDIA LINKS
Facebook: Angel B.
Facebook Fan Page: Romantic Erotic Stories
Twitter: Author Angel B.
Website: Free Your Mind To Books
Amazon Author Central: Angel B.